MAY 4 '70

D1316845

A HISTORIAN'S CREED

A HISTORIAN'S CREED

BY

HENRY OSBORN TAYLOR

in

KENNIKAT PRESS/PORT WASHINGTON, N. Y.

A HISTORIAN'S CREED

Manufactured by Taylor Publishing Company   Dallas, Texas

ESSAY AND GENERAL LITERATURE INDEX REPRINT SERIES

TO

THE MEMORY OF MY WIFE

JULIA ISHAM

A LITTLE BOOK

TO

SO GREAT A MEMORY

Preface

I HAVE devoted the greater part of my life to the currents of thought and feeling constituting the history of man's endeavor to realize whatever he has conceived as best. With me endeavor has always made the real human story, since it is the man himself and his true attainment, while any palpable results are seldom in his control and usually extend beyond his ken. The tale manifests itself in all manner of relations and continuities, physical and spiritual. To my mind it carries the purport and meaning of the world and is the least ambiguous expression of the will of God.

This little volume contains lifelong acceptances, now my final conclusions. The first chapter stresses the continuity of the individual in himself; the second traces continuities in history; the third considers the effect of personal choice and approval upon cosmic conceptions and the consciousness of self; the fourth is an imaginative illustration of these principles in the person of an ancient poet, and the fifth applies them to a fairly definite historical period. Of these chapters the third is the work of the last few months and has not been printed; the first and fourth were published in the *Atlantic Monthly*, and the second in the *American Historical Review*, all quite recently, and the fifth was my Harvard Tercentenary address published in *Speculum, A Journal of Mediaeval Studies* and in the Harvard Tercentenary volumes.

Henry Osborn Taylor

NEW YORK
April, 1939

Contents

I

CONTINUITY AND SURVIVAL

I

Continuity and Survival

I

HOW FAR does the past enter into and become and be part of the present? This query may be put as to the universe or as to the earth and all terrestrial nature. It may be put as to the human race or some portion of it. It may be put as to an individual.

If the past be divided into minute temporal cross sections, any present will consist almost entirely of its immediate past, and the preceding present likewise of its immediate past. But we know that changes have occurred and that the earth and all that lives upon it offer a different aspect from a hundred million years ago; also that the human race is not the same as it was in comparatively recent times, and that an individual alters every moment. It is an obvious inference that no past and present are the same; while, on the other hand, the close approximation of each momentary past to its directly succeeding present indicates a continuity of process from the remotest period. This continuity, as Whitehead urges, is carried into the future by the very nature — the creativity — of the present. That is to say, every present is an activity which presses forward into its immediate future: fastens the future to itself and to some extent determines what it is to be.

Can one segregate the past into currents of causative antecedents with respect to any given event? The "present" of the universe has the whole inclusive past as its antecedent, and I see no objection to adding the word "causative." The present of our earth has for its past whatever the earth has been, and also whatever concurrent factors may have shaped it. These extend beyond the solar system through the stellar universe perhaps with diminishing cogency. The present of the human race upon the earth looks first to a phylogenetic past of men and organisms passing into man. But the effect of the whole terrestrial environment upon this course of evolution must be included, and the influence of the sun and of what stars besides. So the present of a living man, besides some confusedly discerned lines of ancestry, embraces as its past whatever helped to make those very numerous forbears what they were.

With the individual, as with the universe, it is the immediately antecedent phase that most completely corresponds with and constitutes his present, which in turn lays its tentacles upon the future close at hand. The individual's past falls into divisions according to degrees of cogent and direct antecedence. Such divisions, however, are for convenience' sake, and do not imply either essential difference or mutual exclusiveness. Many factors might fall in one division as well as another. I call them natural, historical, social, and individual. "Natural" refers to the whole antecedent past, in the course of which some doubtful lines of ancient organisms evolved and developed until rudimentary men, and finally *homo sapiens*, emerged, with a human brain.

The historical past of the race, and so of our individual, is the last chapter of the story. Its brief course shows little physical change in man, but enormous cultural development. It is a tale of slow beginnings, and then of the checkered progress — or process — of civilization. Does the period indicate a growth of intrinsic mental faculty? "Intrinsic" is the questionable word. The historical period brought incalculable experience to the race; and experience seems to turn to faculty, and thus become part of the most veritable mental growth we know of. Human life combines the mental with the physical. The historical period can hardly be denied its biologic effect upon mankind.

A third division of an individual's total past is the "social" — the constant effect upon him of the family, the tribe, the class group, or the more widely coördinated nation. Such influences affecting our individual are of historical growth and trail their antecedents. They are history in its present impact.

These natural, historical, and social factors, through which is cast the genesis of the individual, will not cease to work upon him through his life. Under their influence the resultant self will progress and grow, constantly absorbing its prior stages. One may think of this self as an association of the coöperating and mutually conditioning psychic and physical faculties forming the whole man. While it is not easy to imagine them functioning in one and the same act, they are connected and interdependent. All of them are disciplined by their prior activities. These prior activities enter into our faculties as elements of aptitude and growth, and also form an admonishing background for future conduct. Needless to say, this background is itself enfolded in an unlimited concourse of antecedents and concomitants. There is no discontinuity; an identity, or core of identity ever growing, maintains itself. Earlier stages are carried on within this process, which is an unbroken becoming — *ein Werdendes*.

II

Such a conception of a self follows the current views of nature, wherein science finds process and ever process, but makes no denial of a reality within the unceasing activities discerned. Be it far from me to deny a continuing reality within the living process making the man. It is hard to think of change without something that changes, of thought without a thinker, or of consciousness without a self. If I can find a physical or physiological continuity behind me, I am more directly assured of a continuing vital and spiritual oneness — that I am still the child, the youth, the man, that I have been. Thoughts and feelings which were me so ardently in my earlier life still work. They were my immediate experience and continue as elements in my faculties. They are more than memories. My parents' care and love live still in me and my responsive love

— a responsiveness which has been mine through life. I recognize the early curiosities roused by people and by whatever flew or ran or crawled. Love of nature's beauties, her clouds and sunsets, her marvelous growths, was a passion that has never left me. I note my youthful impatience ever for wider ranges of study — it has always been my foible to seek to compass too much. My first attempts to formulate my ideas and the substance of my studies come back to me. These early essays are still me, and so are the books which followed on and on. The legal discipline involved in writing my *Treatise on the Law of Private Corporations* (1882–1884) continues. The convictions finding voice in *Ancient Ideals* (1886–1896) are still mine, merely modified in their concrete pointings. Nor have the efforts put into my later work lost their effect. These energies of thought and feeling were not merely experiences of the time, but were to prove lasting extensions of the mind.

There is passion in all intellectual labor. These books were not the fruit solely of mental effort and enlarging scholarly equipment. They issued from a purpose involving my whole nature. Religious faith was in them, and love of art, of every form of harmony perfected in power. My life helped to fashion them, a life which from boyhood always was in love with some living embodiment of loveliness.

The loves and griefs and eventual fulfillment of these elements of my nature were never, as it were, one part of me, while my work was another. Everything worked together to put life in my books and direct my more personal devotions. The gift of loving has never fallen from me, although modifying with the decades, like other natural powers.

The catholic effect of the general factors of human evolution enters the constitution of each individual; but, out of whatever matrix of causation he has sprung, he will carry on his individuality. Resulting from such a manifold of influence, his nature will hold a universality of effect, and will continue as a unified result of all the currents it absorbs. It will never be fully represented by any phase of thought or feeling. Yet its moving pivot will be the conscious nucleus set momentarily upon a present activity of experience.

The self holds types of character and feeling as well as ways of thought which become habits. An integrating force, when it exists, will be a central personal purpose, tending to become clearer and to broaden in requirement and scope. It may absorb the man's entire facultative nature, make his conduct consistent, and give unity to his life.

Not every strong purpose is to be commended — not that of the miser or of the man who drives all things into the net of his personal aggrandizement. A criterion is needed, and perhaps may be found in the history of the human race. This offers various lessons, not easily reconciled. But it points to the building up of societies both as a fact accomplished and as an end to be desired — family, tribe, eventually nations. The last, with all their horrors — call them shortcomings — are the present obvious means of promoting the welfare of their millions. The purposes of individuals should be such as can be carried out with benefit, or without preponderating ill, to others. No individual can live by himself or for himself alone.

Thus the commendable purpose is one that may bring some spiritual or material good to others, in such way as to promote the harmonious conduct of society and make for reasonableness and persuasion. The dominance of these qualities over violence and compulsion is a goal not to be lost sight of, however remote or even impossible it seem. A purpose which even in some small particular may make for this should bring peace to him that holds it. Individuality is integrated and life gains oneness through a feeling of justification, however fragmentary or thwarted the actual accomplishment. The human accomplishment is in the endeavor itself, so far as concerns the man. His happiness will be to relate his will to a broader purpose compassing a universal goal. No harm can come to him as he realizes "that to them that love God all things work together for good" — the good which lies in love of the divine will.

III

Whether these thoughts belong to the argument for the continuity of the self from infancy to age, they fall in with any realization of the agencies involved in the making of man. Along with the pressure of all the elements of nature, effective and prophetic forms had continually come into action through the evolution of organisms and the final discipline and cultural growth of the historic centuries, when *homo sapiens* was entering upon his destiny. Throughout there had been progress from lower to more efficient organic forms, with a striking development (in the later geologic periods) of corporeal bases for psychic energies, all pointing to the growth of mind. It is fatuous to find merely material chance or material determinism where the total infinite process proclaims purpose, a purpose making for the increase of mental and emotional energy — a growth of mind or soul. The goal lies in the coming of spiritual harmonies to power and sovereignty. Human ideals have always acclaimed such, though animal rapacity keep the goal but a goal — a Kingdom of Heaven, as it were. The Kingdom of Heaven cannot be stormed; gentleness seems a likelier approach.

And now if it be true that purpose integrates an individual and maintains his identity, is it not clear that the working together of the causes that have produced him and set him on his way is reason enough why his own conscious purpose should conform to the immanent purpose of their action — a purpose pushing ever to more articulate expression through the energies of organic life? Ardent and loving accord with that insistent and determining plan is the supreme and inclusive sanction of his conduct; within it there can be for him no failure.

If the world is atomic, its atoms are related in their action. In the sphere of life, organisms are the units. They are all individual and all mortal. But their conduct is concerned with other organisms and linked to the world at large. The counters with which organic creation makes its moves are mortal individuals.

Mortality is the keynote of life upon the earth. Instead of deploring the passing of individuals, better recognize this principle as the means by which human interest is constantly renewed. An endless life would weary of experiences apparently changing but generically recurrent. Young people maintain the zest. Organisms of mind and body are obviously unsuited to eternity. Be it given us to see this, even through tears of blinding grief.

But something may be saved; part of the perishing is but apparent. The yearnings and convictions of the ages have busied themselves imagining how this can be. Worlds of intangible spirits have been made, helpless, wretched spirits, and then immortal souls. In mortal life, mind usually is occupied with an obviously perishing body. This is so revolting that the mind devises ideal escapes, sets itself to thinking out (alas! so largely through material analogies) the immortal life of a disembodied soul, an *anima separata*. Is this whole tale a vast futility?

There are no isolated deeds, "dead and done with" when once they have taken place. Every act has indefinite relations and unlimited repercussions. There is no end to any fact; such seems the dynamic make-up of the universe. The corpse of a man passes into untracked combinations. But organic evolution has clearer pointings, showing the continual emergence of psychic faculties in bodies better adapted to their exercises. The mental elements push forward, enlarging their scope and becoming more distinctive. They are still mainly occupied with the demands of the body. Yet in savagery as well as through civilization there will always be a remnant in whom the exercise of mind is of supreme value. Such men are intellectual lights to themselves and their spiritual kin. They advance religion, philosophy, ethics, science, and art. The course of organic evolution issuing in *homo sapiens*, followed by the tragically checkered history of civilization, looks to an eventual dominance of mind, and may justify the hope of a social state of sympathy and mutual understanding, friendship and love. These are not utterly visionary words for those who think in millennia rather than in centuries.

There is causal linkage between one stage of the universe and the next; likewise in a human society, where disorders as well as harmonies are carried on. The clearest survival value is with the latter. Without coördination and coöperation of elements within, and an adjustment with whatever impinges from without, the society will perish.

In the individual there is coöperation among bodily functions, and among apparently psychic qualities. The inner balance has also to relate itself to the physical and social environment, and work out this further adaptation. If the individual be thoughtful and contemplative, one whose mind pushes on to broader consideration, his mental peace will insist upon further ideal linkages and adjustments. He seeks a concord with the whole world and the power moving it. His emotional nature is involved in the urge to place himself within this ideal peace. He must endow its ordainer with those qualities which have spurred him on to long for it — will and purpose, beneficence and love. His own broadest impulse and purpose will be fixed in the love of God and the divine purpose. This is the supreme integrating power in an individual life. It maintains continuity and potently carries on. It is life's consummation and its own reward in the bringing of blessedness. That which is at one with the divine has clearest survival value and the fairest prospect. The obvious fact that the composite organism has run its course need not weaken the conviction that what is fit to survive will not perish. The love of God may be saved in the Eternal Beloved.

IV

There is another way to these conclusions. Life has progressed upon the earth through the evolution of organisms moving toward a more complex efficiency. Mental advance is discerned with the growth of the instrumental bodily parts. In the later geologic periods this advance is so marked as to indicate that the end of organic evolution is the production of mind — which may be accepted as the purpose immanent throughout.

The living organism recoils from whatever threatens it with death or injury; the conscious part of this recoil is fear. But are organisms, as we know them, the final end of the divine purpose? Can the life of mind, toward which they point, be fully realized in them? For example, is it possible for any society of men and women to attain the goal envisaged in their own highest ideals? The needs and passions of the body block the path, the grosser, grasping factors incarnate in the most intelligent and high-minded people. Rage, fighting, war, all manner of violence, are organic in our animal bodies, whatever power of mind they press into their service. Perhaps they can pass away only with the disruption of the animal body. Driven by material interests and impervious to the lessons of the World War, civilized nations are arming to the teeth against each other. And within each nation social groups struggle angrily for a larger share of wealth. Societies ruled by sweet reason and persuasion may not be merely remote but logically impossible for organisms whose bodily needs are unquenchable. I do not press this query, but turn from it to seek a clearer path through the emergent dissolution of the organism.

Well I know that this will bring us back to the immortal discussion of a soul logically and in reality capable of surviving the body. Biology and physics at present afford scant support for any such hypothesis. Modern psychology also goes into the negative scale. And the alleged communications with spirits of the dead are pitiable. I believe no message has ever come across the grave. Is there any direct evidence of the survival of the spiritual parts of human nature? The favoring arguments lack a tangible basis. They rest upon a sense of ideal proprieties. In this respect they resemble all those reasonings of the soul which are fashioned by desires or aspirations of the thinker's nature. An outstanding example is the conception of the plenitude and continuity of the world — the chain of being — which from Plato's time largely dominated the philosophical, religious, and poetic thought of western Europe.[1]

Yet for our purpose such arguments have a negative and a positive justification. The negative lies in our ignorance of fundamental truths or principles. Despite actual and prospective triumphs, science continues to furnish only facts of the middle distances, nor does it promise the solution of any vital problem. We still speculate on fundamentals. The positive justification is in the principle that rational consideration holds the ultimate criterion of what is true or real for man. Intellectual consistency, thinkability, is the final test not only of belief, opinion, conviction, but of the acceptability of the facts of direct observation. To-day a task of physics is to set its results in mathematical equations.

So fundamental ignorance leaves room for speculation on some sort of psychic survival, of which the positive test will be its rational thinkability. I have no novel arguments to offer, and must admit that what are valid or hopeful proprieties to me may be vaporish to others. Psychic survival at all events brings no clear break in continuity, since the qualities fit to survive started with the organism's birth, if not before. But, since fitness and general propriety are the pith of our argument, we may at once reject the survival claim of whatever is not fit. The lower animals are barred out, and even the hordes of men

[1]See the interesting work of Arthur O. Lovejoy, *The Great Chain of Being* (Harvard University Press, 1936).

and women, so called, that have passed away or are now busied ignobly on the earth. Yet perhaps *Dis aliter visum*.

Some pages back I spoke of the indefinite mass of factors going into the making of a man and contributing to the self that asserts itself throughout his organic life — the total self, if that notion is permissible. This is the psychobodily self in full relationship with the sum of organic life, including the impulses of our physiological make-up. Such impulses, feelings, emotions, as well as the man's more distinctly mental activity, all come under the changing focus of consciousness. It is not thinkable that this total organic self can survive the breakup of the body, or pass over as a whole into a disembodied or impersonal existence. And since consciousness, and indeed self-consciousness, may focus upon each and any of these elements during organic life, one may assume some diminution of its range when loosed from the stimulations of the body in our supposed psychic survival. As those stimulations emphasized the sense of self, they tended to turn consciousness into self-consciousness.

On the other hand, the more distinctively mental faculties may be fully active with no consciousness of self. Unimpeded intellectual labor is conscious of its train of thinking, while thought of self is nonassertive, dim, or absent. Whatever may be the vital basis of such thinking, self-consciousness seems to have no part. Moreover, some of our noblest impulses, especially those not directly relating to our body or individual welfare, may be free from self-consciousness. They may temporarily rise to a pitch of selfless devotion to a cause or to another human being. Such unimpeded thinking or devoted conduct is happiness at the time, and comforts us in meditative recall.

Thus, while organic experience calls for some sort of basis in a self, self is forgotten as the mind becomes absorbed in creative thought or the contemplation of a mental panorama. Is it not conceivable that thought and contemplation may persist without consciousness of self when the mortal organism is dissolved? And even though animal impulses have ceased, possibly their effect may carry on in thoughts once springing from them. Our argument, whatever be its value, points to the conclusion that thought will be less impeded when the body's strident claims, with their stirrings of self-consciousness, assert themselves no more. Thought will then become clearer, benevolent impulse more absolute, and the love of God take on a purer glow. Such is the thinkable result of emergent dissolution.

II

CONTINUITIES IN HISTORY

II

Continuities in History

I

CONVINCING arguments are hardly to be looked for in an essay upon the influences and conditions bringing some degree of linkage and expectedness to history; for opinions will depend on temperament and the slant of individual interest in different phases of human life. A writer is likely to win approval only from people more or less like-minded with himself. And with regard to so many-sided a topic, other views may be as valid as the argument contained in the following pages. Even the prospect of the discussion recalls difficulties in the conception of cause, which philosophers since the days of Hume, as well as our recent physicists, have been trying to get around. I hope to avoid them by speaking of "necessary antecedent," "needful preparation," or "enabling or suitable conditions." These terms, when applied to history, carry no implication of strict determinism. They leave place for the action of free and living agencies by reason of whose intervention any historical event appears as a composite and imperfectly predictable result.

Grounded in human nature, the thoughts and acts of men are roused and shaped by their physical and spiritual environment. Men are also moved to think and feel and act by their heritage from the past, which is part of their education and contributes to their knowledge. Save for its discipline and teaching they would not have the thoughts they entertain or a good part of their feelings; nor could they construct or create whatever they are engaged upon. The influence of the past blends with that of the working and insistent environment; but neither one nor the other, nor their combined effect, wholly constrains the emerging present upon which they act. For in every present the energies of living men are apt to fashion to new forms whatever affects them or comes within the circle of their interest.

The growth of dogmatic Christianity illustrates these principles. It rested on the teachings of Jesus and his Apostles, as understood and accepted by their adherents and those who came after them. Current ways of feeling and thinking in the eastern Mediterranean affected and became a part of the interpretation and manner of acceptance of these teachings. Belonging to a notably reasoning world, the early Christians sought to understand their faith in a manner acceptable to their reason. More specifically the will to rationalize the Faith and the method of its rational formulation came from the later cosmopolitan phases of Greek philosophy.

But antecedents and accompanying conditions did not create the Nicene formulation or wholly determine what it was to be. The creeds were gradually formed by the Greek and Latin Fathers, from Tertullian on through

Origen, Athanasius, and Augustine. These men were affected by current thinking and worked in the medium of their own preparation and accepted past, which gave substance and method to their thought. But they were constructive minds and not mere recipients of what they used. Nor did they reproduce the past either piece by piece or in its whole composite nature. Even what they accepted as the divine word they shaped in their understanding.

The same may be said of the cumulative scholastic reformulation of the patristic achievement. Its apex, the *Summa theologiae* of Thomas Aquinas, was the work of that great schoolman, although he could not have composed it without the aid of all that made up his education and his past, including the substantial philosophy of Aristotle, which the Fathers had not used.

II

Recalling the phrases "needful antecedents" and "enabling conditions," I would now say that "continuities" refer to physical conditions and the persistent human qualities which have shaped the role of mankind upon the earth. The activities of these qualities fluctuate and yet exert influences more or less constant throughout the succession of forms produced or assumed by them. Although our continuities reach back to include whatever has contributed to set *homo sapiens* upon the stage, we shall be occupied mainly with human tendencies and active faculties.

It may be well to start with the primordial fact that the universe remotely and permissively and the sun more directly have produced and still maintain an earth suited to the sustenance of living organisms. Branching from this base, our continuities would consist, first, of the physical environment of land and air and water existing and operative beneath and within the living garment of plants and animals. Next, the plants and animals afford a ceaselessly active and formative environment for each other. This living system, which embraces the human race, maintains itself through universal and reciprocal consumption, assimilation, and adaptation. Never stable, always undergoing change, it is an immortal living continuity.

The elemental and organic orders of continuity carry ingredients that enter human nature and qualities which men share with other animals. Yet there is place for a third order consisting of the more characteristic qualities of mankind. These act with some volitional freedom and unpredictability. Constantly active, they manifest themselves in a variety of forms that change. And, more than all other animals and plants, men hasten the changes in their threefold environment of elemental nature, plants and animals, and other tribes of men. The whole story of the earth's use and consumption, the action of men upon plants and animals and upon other human groups, the increase of population and growth of nations, the encroachment of cities upon the country, and countless other facts attest the effects of human agencies upon human environments.

Organisms have many ways of conforming means and

ends with respect to their environment and within themselves. They are individual systems of assimilation and adaptation. Acts of an organism normally make for its benefit. Each incident of functioning is teleological, has an aim. A functional act may be said to carry on and have a quality of continuity. It is never merely in and of itself, but has linkage through its aim and the aims of its antecedents. This teleological linkage extends to the relations among organisms and reaches backward indefinitely. Much of the functioning of the human organism has a limited physiological aim. In conscious action the aim enlarges and may extend beyond the organism in space and time and consideration of consequences.

If the functioning of organisms is aimful, one is tempted to find a continuing purposiveness running through the whole process and even directing it. Such a purpose cannot be merely antecedent to the incidents of its fulfillment but continues as a factor within the scheme of things. The object need not be an end ultimately to be reached in time. It may lie within the process and its character be inferred from what is observed. The evidence of such a purpose seems to me everywhere, though many minds are closed to it. My own conviction is built up from my life's experience, a synthetic conclusion doubtless colored by individual temperament.[1] In turn my thinking is unified through this conviction, which nevertheless is partly intuitive since its universality transcends the range of con-

[1] Such a conviction may be called a "conceptual scheme," like "evolution." A conceptual scheme tends to unify thinking.

crete evidence. I go further and call it the divine purpose and am willing to look on my conviction as an act of faith.

I find an analogy in the botanist's or zoölogist's acceptance of evolution. His total knowledge and his reason convince him that the succession of organisms from the simpler to the most complex has come about through what he calls evolution. He cannot define the process and is far from knowing the manner of its action or how it has taken place, though he discerns contributing factors. His conviction goes beyond definite evidence and is thus a faith, like my belief in a divine purpose. This kind of faith is not limited to such large matters but enters generally into our knowledge. A partly intuitive conviction ordinarily caps and concludes our acceptances or opinions and points our action. No grasp of fact hangs on a single reason. All sorts of previous cognizance take part and yet may prove inadequate for the novel occasion. The decisive intuition comes from the man's total fashioning experience with all the engendered impulses and prejudices.

But to return: if the aim realizes itself within the process, the process may contain its own fulfillment. We are not obliged to envisage some imagined end beyond the process and its time limits. Yet that it carries aim and value within and for itself does not preclude a further eventual end. The visible process may not be the end-all. Growth of mind or spirit through evolving stages is felt by some to indicate extension or survival beyond the physical ingredients.

III

The aimfulness in the conduct of organisms enters the continuities of human history. The latter, through their larger scope and freedom, further exemplify the causal efficacy of the past and the tendency of every antecedent to enter and become part of what it helps to bring about. Past events are never merely antecedent but carry on as factors of the succeeding present and contribute to its energies, conduct, and achievement. Enabling conditions resulting from many lines of antecedents act together in each present.

Except through poetic metaphor or in extreme metaphysics, the processes of inorganic nature are not given psychic qualities. But such are part of living organisms. Doubtful in plants, rudimentary in the humbler animals, no one can say just when and where they became operative. Bound up with them, the beginnings of consciousness offer a like baffling question. But consciousness as well as psychic qualities are evident in mammals; and a striking feature of mammalian evolution has been the growth of the organs through which psychic qualities are manifested, and eventually the higher phases of mentality.

Physical and physiological elements load the prehuman past. But mind was there as well. No need to say that the contents of human history have always been spiritual as well as physical and that both enter into historical continuity.[2] The building up and maintenance of societies are

[2] With me the word "spiritual" is broader than "mental" and includes the feelings and emotions which are not palpably of the body.

a universal feature, and the qualities that enable men to live advantageously together are largely of the mind. The progress of mankind falls in with the pointings of spiritual growth and cannot but conform to the apparent immanent purpose of the factors working together in the evolution of the race.

In human history (as throughout all antecedent evolution) different strains of continuity interlace and pervade each other. An indefinite number of partial causes or enabling conditions unite in the coming to pass of any event. It is not easy to separate them into independent agencies or appraise their several cogencies, for they move through mutual reactions to a convergent result, which may nevertheless contain disruptive elements temporarily brought together.

A directly causative section of the past, which obviously continues in the present, is the race of men or quasi-men and organisms passing into such. The continuity of the race approaches an apparent stability in the transmission of constant or very slowly changing qualities. But one cannot leave out a single factor. Again, nature's processes carry on the past apparently with lavish waste, throwing out a thousand seeds or eggs for one that germinates. Human history likewise carries on its conserving economy through recessions and catastrophes.

While individuals appear as the units of historical continuity, each has been a continuity since birth and is linked with the ranges of antecedents which have made its life possible.[3] They may hand themselves on through their children or the influence of their acts. The latter have aim and value in the doing and continuity in their effect: for instance, a heroic deed, or the making of a work of art, or the composition of a book.

IV

Life holds the aimfulness of creative evolution. It is the trunk that branches and flowers in the activities of men. Each individual presses to fulfill his nature and feel it to the full, as when he satisfies his hunger or sex lust, adorns his body, slays for very rage or to show himself foremost and win his group's acclaim. Fame will extend his life and deeds. The urge to self-fulfillment is in the man of intellect as well, poet, philosopher, scientist, each moving along the path of his faculties and vocation. Nor has such a one lost the desire to show himself the man he is.

The acts of men are instinctive, habitual, passionate, or consciously intended. The urge of life is in them all. Yet by reason of life's unfailing spontaneity, each present moment works a change in whatever comes to it. Because it is alive, a society or an individual acts in its own way upon every proffered influence. Always undergoing change, the physical and spiritual experience which has formed the race and become part of its faculties passes on, together with the material civilization, which is the shell. But since buildings, aqueducts, and cornfields have effec-

---

[3] See the preceding essay, "Continuity and Survival."

tive being only in their use, their transmission hangs upon the human factors. All stand and fall together. If monumental structures remain for the admiration of future ages, that hardly renews the life of these substantial ghosts.

Judging by noise and flare, the greater part of what thus passes on has arisen from material needs. Life in the flesh, with its vehemence, greed, and rancor, holds the stage, makes wars, builds houses, overthrows societies. It is partly fashioned by conceptions of the mind. Evolution is always pointing to the last. But mentality never looks big. Human life is so wrapped up in the needs and passions of the animal that only a warped and driven course seems left to mind. Yet mind leads in survival value and survival power. Its efficiency tends to center in a few. All civilization is an affair of remnants, through whom pass the grains of truth that fit the ways of life imperishably: grains of goodness, of aloofness from the ways of crass destruction.

Human beings differ in strength of volition and the control of their lives: the spontaneous self-directing power of the human personality. Often the press of circumstances seems to hem in a life or, much less frequently, to favor its freer expansion. Obviously most lives are fashioned by the suggestions or compulsions of environment. A minority reach out beyond. A high degree of conceptual and sometimes actual freedom is his who forms a comprehensive plan of life and is able to pursue it.

Life's energies and fundamental impulses manifest themselves in forms that pass, yet not without effect. Discontinuity in history is an illusion. More real is the overlapping of thought and feeling through the succession of forms, which have effective continuity in their influence upon what follows them. The human faculties expressing themselves in these forms are affected by the experience and discipline, and press on to create what is never a sheer duplicate and may appear quite different from its preparatory antecedents. And the forms themselves, although products of the past, may continue active in the present. Such living forms are the laws and customs of our society and government, and indeed the whole structure and content of our culture. All this is the formative part of our present as well as the material upon which its energies work fruitfully. Thus the passing forms share in the continuity of the faculties of which they are the manifestation.

In this way each phase of any human institution, social, legal, or political, has part in the genesis of its successor, however different that may show itself. The successor may appear as a reaction against a way of living or social adjustment that the society has tired of. But whatever arises is still related to former experience and the abilities thereby acquired. Examples of all kinds strew human history; they obviously make up the story of institutions. The British parliament is an outstanding illustration. Less patently convincing may be the Roman republic in its lessening efficiency from the time of the Gracchi, with the impotent fury of its final period passing through dictatorships to the establishment of an imperial rule where still flitted the ghosts of republican institutions. The empire took form from these as much as from pressing exigencies.

Like principles appear in the figurative arts and indeed in the progression of all products of human ingenuity; even in the humbler utensils of domestic living or machinery where the discarded expedient brings the new improvement. The earlier pattern and the discipline gained by its production affect the nature of its supplanter. A similar combination of enabling influence works more subtly in sheer intellectual activity. The conduct of the rational faculties, expressing themselves in successive modes of thought, makes up the history of philosophy. Or for another example, the tendency to rationalize in apologetic allegories unites with those serpent forms to produce strange children.[4]

All such effects and linkages are strengthened by the force of habit and the drag of custom. Habit, whether mental or manual, gives body to the impulse to think, feel, and behave in well-worn grooves. The accepted fitness of constantly recurring notions and the utility of actions oft repeated, and so made easier, tend to prevent scrutiny.

[4] For decency's sake thoughtful Greeks, even in the fifth century B.C., turned the scandalous doings of the Homeric gods into natural myths, a method accepted by the religious conservatism of the Stoics. The Hellenizing Jew Philo used allegory to make Genesis a vehicle of Greek moral philosophy at the opening of the Christian era. Through further and new-found allegories the Fathers made the contents of the Old Testament prefigurative of the truth of Christ and softened its crudities to suit the pagan conscience. In the Middle Ages, when apologetic needs were no longer pressing, allegorical interpretation was taken as a matter of course. It was applied to the Mass as well as to the parts and ornaments of cathedrals; it was used in political argument and pervaded popular medieval literature (*Roman de la rose*). Symbolical meanings were accepted as expressing the deepest truth of God's purpose in creation. See *The Mediaeval Mind*, chs. XXVIII and XXIX.

Custom seems to imply the loyalty of conduct to venerated motives. It holds to the old ways, disliking and fearing change. In their very nature, habit and custom are strong conserving continuities.

Imitation is allied with them. It is instinctive in young animals. Fawns follow the cautious doe with riveted attention and imitate her every movement for safety's sake. Imitation is habitual with children and an efficient means of their education. Through it come speech and wiser conduct. It soon discloses a variety of motives. There may be emulation in a child imitating another's play. Youths and maidens are moved to keep in fashion and emulate an admired rival. Vanity and the desire to shine have entered. In the arts and crafts pupils imitate a teacher to gain his skill; from ethical motives disciples imitate a holy man. In such cases, though instinct or habit survive, imitation has become a part of rational conduct.

Imitation is not originative or progressive in itself. Whether it is a conservative influence depends on what is imitated. To follow innovations either blindly or upon consideration is not conservative. Yet, with these provisos, imitative thought and conduct may be put with habit and custom among the unprogressive continuities in history. Even beyond the range of their influence, through all provinces of desire and endeavor there is connection and causal sequence, sometimes through reaction or repulsion. The earlier phase may be a springboard to jump from, and the jump reaches that much further. Currents of influence are not dependent on the survival of individuals. Rather they keep fresh and vivid because old men and women die, while young minds and bodies carry on with the energy of youth, its enterprise and its imagination: "Oh! brave new world," cries Miranda. "'Tis new to thee," replies Prospero.

v

The living body is a functional process which feels itself most surely in its pains and strident needs. Its cravings urge on the organism's psychic phase, which is the mind. That also is an activity: in functioning it is itself. Action animates and delights it. In this lies the mind's exhaustless happiness. It is always looking for the interesting and the apt, which when found stings and pricks it on. Its history is the story of a quest as manifold as comprehensive. Each perception, each rational insight, each leap of intuition, every desire with its love of what it feels the need for — all are releases of the energy inherent in the mind. Also they open new vistas of the quest. And when the mind looks within, it may discover that it has itself pointed the search and shaped the sought-for fulfillment to the form of an imagined best. The quest takes many paths, along which the mind is urged by its impulses, its modes, its faculties. The paths are the mind's attributes in action.

The unceasing activities of human minds constitute the spiritual continuity of history. But a society has no common mind any more than a common body. Mental activity is always that of an individual. Yet its manifestations may be drawn forth and shaped by the common need of men to live together and by currents of like thoughts and feelings producing uniformity of concern and temper.

VI

Within the main trunk of life the urge of sex is a vital continuity. Not merely does it propagate mankind, but its repercussions and emotions, and sentiments flowering in love, prompt noble as well as violent conduct and animate all forms of poetry and art. No need to touch this boundless story.[5] We pass to another main continuity of history, the manifold urge to form and maintain societies. Though the basis be the body's needs, there enters the impulse of the human spirit to profit from fellow feeling and intercourse.

Mankind's responding efforts make a large part of history. They have been credited to the "social instinct." Certainly man is or has become a social animal. But the endeavor for a communal life has had a variety of motives. The behavior of other animals is indicative. Some sort of living together is the rule; the solitary life is difficult and rare. With ants and bees coöperation has resulted in specializing not only their behavior but their structure. With lives reduced to fixed functions, they have become sheer parts of a social organism.[6] But in the case of birds and

[5] At the close of the next essay, p. 82 sqq., love is spoken of as the builder of the self and its world.

[6] The caste system of India points in a like direction; but no caste has become incapable of sharing in the propagation of the race.

mammals the formation of groups seems to depend on the particular need of protection and the manner of getting food. Migratory birds flock when migrating, but not during the mating season. Herbivorous quadrupeds herd together for safety. Birds of prey live and hunt singly or in couples, which is the way with lions, tigers, and leopards. Wild dogs and wolves, but not foxes, hunt in packs. Among the primates, baboons and monkeys may live in troops, but the great apes, who can take care of themselves, appear not to form groups beyond the family, and pass part of their lives alone. Thus these apes who are nearest to man show scant communal life, and a survey of other animals hardly points to any universal "social instinct."

To what extent our apelike or manlike ancestors lived in companies is not clear. Different circumstances would breed different habits. But *homo sapiens* at an early stage somehow realized the advantages of groups for hunting and defense and later for a division of labor. Life in communities would foster habits of mutual dependence and promote the growth of social qualities. At all events the trend toward some kind of association has been universal. The particular social forms spring from and again produce the character of the group — the complex of feeling and intelligence. They arise as well from the impacts of environment, natural and human. It would be rash to ascribe preponderant effect to one or the other of these factors, since they are interdependent. Changes in the human or natural elements will modify the social structure, and new needs may pattern it anew, but the urge to maintain a society works on within those changing forms.

The qualities promoted through social living look to the satisfaction of the individual as a member of society. They would enhance his life by attracting the favor of his fellows. Then comes the wish to direct or otherwise influence the conduct of the social complex. Vanity and emulation are examples of those qualities which crave appreciation, praise, and sympathy. Upon their gratification the man responds with affectionate esteem and sympathy. Such qualities are part of the impulse and desire of every individual to exalt and express himself, a desire which cannot but be social in its fulfillment. A man does not talk merely to make known his thought or feeling or intention. Usually he wishes to show the sort of man he is. There is feeling in the impulse to express oneself, and feeling accompanies every communication. Clearly the urgency of self-expression and the desire to impart one's thoughts and feelings are among the continuities of history.

Perhaps owing to some pervasive similarity both in physical environment and human nature, certain types of social organization constantly recur, especially with respect to the exercise of authority in a society. Conditions of flight compel migrating geese to have a leader and keep to a certain pattern while flying. Somehow the strongest wolf becomes the leader of the hunt. The great apes apparently have no leaders, and leadership is hard to find among primitive men. It emerges with the development of the social structure. Less pronounced in small primitive groups, it reaches a harsh absoluteness in larger aggregates, and not merely among savages. Ancient records of civilization disclose the king or pharaoh supreme, though his power necessarily finds limitations in military and executive requirements. Moreover assassination lurks, and revolt may overthrow the tyrant. This fairly universal and absolute kingship includes the office of high priest, who has paramount authority to placate and move the god, for the efficiency of social organization is linked to gods and demons and the means of moving or restraining them. Everywhere ceremonies raise the king above his subjects and guard his royal high-priestly functions.

Kingships, tyrannies, dictatorships have so prevailed in history as to lead one to regard them as an essential feature of the urge to maintain a social structure, and so as a historical continuity. Yet they have been broken into by repeated attempts to establish other ways of ordering a people through a ruling class or the people themselves. Springing from impulses of self-assertion, this counter tendency has not been marked in Asiatic countries, where the insistence of the individual is weak. It sprang to life in the old Greek cities, mightily proved itself in the Roman republic, and has persisted in England. It may foster sentiments of social freedom and equality.

These counter efforts may aim at democracy and representative government, with universal suffrage as their ideal. But history seems to show, for instance in the story of Rome, that the more widely authority is distributed among the people the less effectively it will be exercised. A frequent result is reversion to a personal autocratic leadership, in practice if not in theory. The only lasting endeavor for a liberal or representative government is found in Great Britain and the nations springing from her. Perhaps Holland, Switzerland, and the Scandinavian countries should be added. We in the United States, nurtured in this liberal tradition, do not realize the limited area of its successful operation. We regard what has taken place in continental Europe since the World War as deplorable occurrences, almost accidents. A clearer view shows how unprepared and unfit for a representative or liberal order were the Germans or the quite dissimilar Italians, not to mention Spain and Russia, whose incapacities for self-government are as different as they are insurmountable.

It seems to be another tendency of societies to gravitate into classes. One may imagine these to have arisen in the obscure past through the inequalities of individuals shown in diversities of temper, aptitude, and faculty, tending to shake down into class distinctions. Environment and circumstance also have worked their differentiating role. Part of the people may have come from elsewhere, perhaps brought in as slaves. A nation usually is a conglomerate. The growth of special characteristics in each class may be traced, while the origins baffle us. But in view of the almost universal existence of classes one hesitates to ascribe them to any particular diversity of circumstance and situation.

VII

Although human qualities do not always work in harmony, they all contribute to the making and undoing of societies. Religion, an unfailing element in the social effort, likewise draws upon all sides of human nature. The religious impulse and imagination may sound in feeling, yet the religious mind is not indifferent to other modes of understanding fact. A synthesis of thought and feeling takes form from the man's experience and courts the support of any pertinent evidence.

Religion was mentioned with kingship. Properly enough, since the want of a king is related to religious longing. Self-reliance comes tardily to men. While the primitive uses his own strength and quick perceptions, he is beset with fear of things about him. Such baneful motives as he feels within him he imputes to animals and trees or imagines indwelling spirits. All of which, with his felt need of protection, is as natural to him as the cast of a stone. Discrimination slowly brings some order to this crass confusion. But the longing for aid persists. Homer's heroes sense the help or opposition of a god at every step. Hopes and fears regarding superhuman beings pervade all history. Man's dependent linkage with them makes the religious frame, whatever features the picture within it may take on.

But there is more to religion. Man's world from the beginning is shadowed in mystery. He is always hankering after the veiled significance. This is a religious phase that

quickly turns visible things to symbols and devises allegories. Progress lies in a subtler and generalized conception of what is beyond sense. Among capable peoples
thoughts of the gods unify. The gods become God. Thus
the religious intelligence works its way to an idea of divine
order and control, which is never the naked creature of
reason but is clothed and colored by feeling. Intuition,
emotion, reverence, and sometimes love give wings of
faith to the understanding. The sense of God and the divine control may take shape as belief in a benevolent
providence, which in turn may become intimately personal in its loving care of every man and woman and
prove the salvation of the responsive soul. It was the historical office of Christianity to bring to pass this revelation
of the divine and human heart.

It is hard to say how much the earliest stages of religion
had to do with the behavior of men toward each other.
Yet as tribal life gives rise to common interests and re-
quires adjustments, religion becomes tribal and concerns
itself with conduct. It has regard for the social order and
sets its sanction on proper social behavior. Only in society
can the individual complete his nature. Likewise through
concern for society and the right conduct of its members,
religion wins through to its noblest forms.

Animal sacrifices have been a common means of pro-
pitiating the gods. More spiritual conceptions of the divine
bring other thoughts of reconcilement, as it is perceived
that God desires justice rather than sacrifice. Divine favor
rests with righteous houses. So religion and ethics advance

together. Both lay stress upon motive and intent, and thought sets itself to distinguish the better and the rational from the irrational and worse. But discrimination is impressed with desire. The eager aim presents itself as a good reason for the act — a principle covering impulsive, thoughtless acts and those of conscious purpose. The desire and the aim tend to justify the act. There is little intentionally wrong conduct among men, since everyone is apt to think his action justified. This applies only too obviously to acts of violence in social excitement. Nor is it far from the opinion of Socrates and Plato that no one does wrong knowingly, or even from the words of Jesus, "Father forgive them for they know not what they do."

But I should make another approach to this conclusion. Aim and endeavor inhere in life itself: life is endeavor. Its aim must be at what is felt or deemed desirable — perhaps mistakenly. Biologically there is no evil aim. The principle of endeavor, which is a main continuity of history, brings a leaven of reconciliation to the opposite aims of different individuals. The element of endeavor, which is life, was in them all.

Thus humanity, moved by impressions of the physical world, turns to beliefs that are termed religious. Ethical discrimination proceeds. These phases of feeling and mentality, though manifested in forms that change and pass, constitute historical continuities.

VIII

The arts and crafts are part of human conduct. They also are a morality, though their aim at what is fit and excellent may be limited to the object in hand, for the tendency of endeavor is to do its best — bring its aim to full attainment. This is an inherent principle of craftsmanship. In primitive man it produces improvement in his handmade tools. The earliest pots are crude but the tendency to improve them irresistible: bulges are reduced, curves perfected. The pot becomes more useful, more fit, more pleasing to handle and look at. Very soon it will be intentionally beautified with streaks of pigment. An element of beauty exists in all efficiency; to make this element more pointed through decoration seems also an inherent and immortal impulse in mankind.

The desire to make objects beautiful becomes a dominant motive in the higher ranges of things makeable by the human hand and spirit. It is the inspiration and may be the end and goal of the fine arts. Craftsmanship must keep its practical aim: an architect must bear in mind the purpose of the building. But the building may be clothed with ornament, and properly so long as its usefulness is not impaired. If it have a spiritual purpose, this may aptly be carried to explicit expression, as in the sculpture and painted glass of a cathedral.

Sculpture and painting, even when not serving a practical use, hold to the principle of efficiency in the presentation of whatever may be the subject; that is, they keep to the delineation of the subject itself, which shall not be overladen or obscured or defiled by distracting adornments or accessories. This gives the work of art unity, power, and the final charm of achievement termed beauty. A like principle marks the excellence of poetry. In great poetry, as in great plastic art, unity is equivalent to the ideal. For the ideal is unity attained by omitting whatever is irrelevant to the event or the feeling or the character to be set forth. The lyric will admit nothing impairing its pattern of tone and feeling; the drama will reject whatever distracts attention from its compact plot; and broad as properly may be the epic, it tends to keep to the current and temper of its narrative. These observations may apply also to the excellence of musical compositions.

The arts are modes of significant endeavor and human self-expression. In their ceaseless pursuit of the fit, the efficient, the beautiful, they belong among the continuities of history. No need to characterize their end as the attainment of the beautiful and good. Each of these time-honored terms is a synthesis, transcending analysis or unsuited to its methods.

IX

The motives and endeavors which more especially carry out man's intellectual nature are still to be spoken of. One may place them under intellectual curiosity and the rationalizing faculty. The latter is more universal. Should it be regarded as the tendency to rationalize or the faculty of rationalization? The two phrases have much the same meaning inasmuch as mind is altogether an activity and should not be divided into faculties except for convenience of speech. It is the nature of mind to use its powers. Among them is reason, which tends to exert itself as part of mind and may be regarded either as a tendency or a faculty.

The rational faculty has no special topic or fund of knowledge, but busies itself with whatever is offered for its consideration. There is always a content of knowledge in the mind, with which the rational faculty may compare what is freshly presented. But if the fund of knowledge is inapplicable, inactive, or forgotten, the rational faculty may lack data for a sound comparison or fondly disregard whatever checks its course. Hence often in the crude and ignorant past, or the crude and ignorant present, the human tendency to formulate, explain, or rationalize has set itself to vindicate and justify rites and practices and hoary acceptances that are ripe for the discard. It has frequently sought to rationalize phantasies rejected by other modes of grasping or constructing fact, and the rationalization may be more absurd than the custom or acceptance itself. The logical process does not guarantee a reasonable result.

But rationalization may be the most valid of all intellectual operations. It is not easy to go beyond the conclusions of rational consideration when it reviews the work of other human faculties or virtues or predilections and criticizes their methods or results. Rational consideration also seeks to bring its thinking to some ultimate conclusion, and, though no topic belongs to it especially, it has an object peculiar to itself, even that end or quality of ultimate conclusion which is reason's goal. The entire history of philosophy is an illustration of the endeavor for ultimate conclusions. When the conclusion relates to being, rational consideration may be called metaphysics, or theology when the conclusion relates to God. When the conclusion concerns observation of the natural world or human conduct or social relations, rational consideration in each case might dub itself the philosophy of the matter.

Ultimate rational consideration, which may be called philosophy, follows the changing times. It applies itself to the chief intellectual interest of one age and then turns to some other preoccupation, representing the absorption of a later epoch. This succession of intellectual interests fills out the history of thought. The rationalizing faculty constructs the forms in which the topics are rationally apprehended or understood. Such forms or categories will change or become outmoded with the passing of intellectual emphasis from one topic to another, but rational consideration continues to function on and on. It discloses the overlappings of thought and feeling from one generation to another, demonstrates their sequential or causal lineage, and even makes their succession appear as part and parcel of its own continuous activity. The intellectual impulse to rationalize is as immortal as the bulkier urge to build societies.

Extremely variegated is the panorama of intellectual interest and emphasis to which rational consideration has been drawn from age to age. The early Greek philosophers, for example, set themselves to construct a rational scheme for their perceptive understanding of the external world. After them Socrates began the dialectic scrutiny of words and concepts, a matter previously ignored. Plato, proceeding further, concludes that ultimate reality dwells in the ideas of the mind. The Stoics and Epicureans shift the interest and effort to human values and conduct. Then, with the faltering of human self-reliance, reason seeks reassurance from the religious intuitions of mortal need. Passing through the metaphysics of Neo-Platonism, it absorbs the alluring phases of Greco-Oriental thought. And when the Mediterranean world turns to Christianity, the insistent philosophic mind undertakes the rational formulation of the Faith. This task advances through the medieval centuries to the final achievement of the *Summa theologiae*. From devotion to theology rational consideration has gained religious feeling, and with this moving aid has built cathedrals, has stamped its thought of God and man on sculpture and painted glass, and expressed itself in the plan and conclusion of Dante's medieval *Commedia* and Milton's Protestant epics.

In the fifteenth and sixteenth centuries the physical world knocked more loudly upon minds previously addicted to reasoning on divine salvation. Geographical discoveries roused bolder thoughts, while a renewed if not novel impulse to observe and study nature threatened reliance on authority. As methodical observation fought its way to recognition, rational consideration — that is, philosophy — began to shift its view and refashion its categories to a more genial reception of observed phenomena. Thereupon appeared the loose but ambitious systems of the South Italians Telesio and Bruno and the Englishman Bacon. As the decades pass, the results of methodical observation are evinced in the quickened progress of astronomy, physics, and biology. In a century or two natural science becomes a dominant practical as well as intellectual interest. At the present time the problem pressing most urgently upon the considering mind is that of the consistency and certainty of this very body of scientific knowledge which has been gained through systematic observation of the natural world. There are also prickly questions as to the validity of the more promiscuously gathered mass of data concerning human relations in societies. By stoutly setting itself to these matters rational consideration carries on its task and proves again that the will to rationalize and reach ultimate conclusions is an immortal historical continuity.

x

The search for knowledge through observation has been more fitful than the inclination to rationalize whatever presses on the mind. All peoples wish to know how to make things and equip their lives profitably. A respectable accumulation of practical knowledge has more than once resulted. Curiosity passes for a mammalian instinct and is universal among mankind. Nevertheless disinterested and insistent intellectual curiosity is far from common. Occasionally it seems to follow upon the practical effort to know, as an ambient flame of unexpended energy. It sprang to action among those same Ionian philosophers who followed "natural philosophy" in the old-fashioned sense. Its broken story appears ever and anon as the converse of rational consideration, which in Hellenic and medieval times ever tended to paralyze any effective impulse to observe nature. This impulse did not enter the mentality of Socrates, and, while Plato was profoundly interested in the cosmos, his intellectual home was the realm of reason. But Aristotle was an observer of nature and a great zoölogist. A like interest touched some of his disciples, although the tendencies of the time were strongly set toward ethics. Yet the following decades brought a marked advance in mathematics and astronomical science, while physiological investigations in Alexandria and other cities added much to the knowledge of the human body. From Alexandrian doctors, as well as from the Hippocratics preceding them, a sound medical tradition carried across the centuries to Galen, himself a remarkable experimenter working in the second century A.D. But soon curiosity as to the actual facts of nature was swamped by theology and its passion for allegory. Observation may be said to have slumbered till Roger Bacon and others awakened it to a false dawn in the thirteenth century. Later, as we have noted, its sun broke through and evoked an ardent and methodical investigation of nature, including man, which was destined to produce the cluster of sciences marking our own time.

On the whole, the acute and effective observation of nature has been confined to European peoples and their progeny. It has not flourished in Africa or Asia, not even in India, where rational consideration has always had its home. Only Japan has nimbly adopted the science of the West. One may therefore doubt whether the record warrants our placing intellectual curiosity or its products among the unfailing continuities of history. The scientific examination of human society is more recent and has but the promise of a child still subject to the round of infantile diseases. Let us not forget, however, that life itself is purpose and endeavor, whether its inherent aimfulness be dumb or conscious and articulate. Intellectual curiosity is one of its loftiest manifestations and therefore has its roots in that which is immortal.

XI

The evolutionary processes resulting in a diversity of organisms and the emergence of mental qualities seem to carry purpose. Such purpose, whether or not conceived as an antecedent cause, is a directive influence within the active scheme of things and possibly may look to a growth of mind beyond the range of physical ingredients. Sequential dependence throughout the evolution of the more complex from the simpler organic forms, as well as the interdependence holding among contemporary organisms, bears a loose analogy to the order of man's physiological and psychic functions, with the animal propensities the earlier. The range of human faculties from the violent to the more rational follows the sequence of evolution and indeed its immanent purpose. All seems to point to the eventual supremacy of those faculties which regard the welfare of the individual as a member of society. To this end the mind may join with its "nobler reason" to restrain its "fury," those animalities which have been so apt to press craft and ingenuity to their service.[7]

Through the past history of man the mind has not been innocent. Yet it has been and still is the home of persuasion and good thought. Its saving function is to bring to dominance the thoughts and feelings which its best consideration may accept. It will thus contribute breadth and balance to the action of its more specific phases. Its total insight and vision will enlighten the faculties working to reform or overthrow societies, enabling them to weigh the respective advantages of custom and innovation; will help to fashion ways of conduct and guide the straining of religious need; will participate in craftsmanship and artistic creation, promoting love of the true, the beautiful, and good. And its all-embracing reasonableness will advise the intellectual faculties of rational consideration and scientific curiosity and unify their quest of knowledge. By thus bringing the action of its various phases under the sovereignty of their united wisdom — their "nobler reason," if one will — the mind attains a peace and concord of its own, in harmony with the purpose immanent in the evolutionary process.

[7] "Yet with my nobler reason 'gainst my fury do I take part." *The Tempest.*

III

THE CHOSEN SELF

III

The Chosen Self

I

THE COSMOS and the human self present themselves as contrasted though, as we hope, friendly opposites. These royal mysteries are the mind's ultimate concern. The cosmos has been thoughtfully considered as a whole; it has been regarded as amenable to rational thinking and as somehow guided and controlled. More fruitfully, perhaps, bits of it have been investigated piece by piece, with recognition of the relatedness of parts, though the roots of things are hidden. The mystery of the self has hitherto proved impregnable to direct attack. No analysis has penetrated the unity of the first person singular: *I* think. Ever changing, yet always identical, the *I* is still unthinkable. Baffled questioners have been driven to say, There is no self. But human thought and conduct seem to imply its existence and indicate its character. It abides as a conviction of consciousness and may be of use in explaining human conduct. What is the self but the very man, whose action or resolve or sustained thought looks to some answering profit or the fulfillment of a norm reflecting his own nature?

Acts issue from the doer, and thought reflects the

thinker. Even where there is no intended self-disclosure in the act and the spoken thought is concerned with outer objects, something of the man is revealed. Heroic conduct is an expression of the hero — as when a man, disabled in struggling through Antarctic snow, turns away from his companions to certain death in the storm to give them a better chance; or Achilles avenges Patroclus, knowing that his own death must follow. Since such resolve and action carry the press of feeling and character, they disclose the man. On the other hand, a course of conduct affects the doer, directs the growth of self. Everyone issues from the womb with a certain equipment of potential faculties pointing to some line of conduct or province of action likely to be taken up, which in the event will tend to fashion the self or character.

More explicitly, the mind is mirrored in some broad scheme of thinking, like the Aristotelian cosmos: in the middle the Earth, with heavy terrestrial things naturally seeking its center, while just as naturally flames rise upwards. In the heavens around the Earth the incorruptible planets, stars, and sun revolve, each fixed in a rigid circle, the outermost circle moved by the All-mover. This scheme, which won the approval of twenty centuries, reflects the mind that constructed it. A different mind appears in the genially imagined cosmos of Plato's *Timaeus*: the universe was framed by a creator who through that goodness which knows no grudge sought to make it in his own image good and beautiful. He made its soul to be the body's sovereign. He made gods by whom the souls of men were fashioned and set in lustful bodies, yet with power to master their bodies' violence and lead righteous lives.

Following suggestions from Aristotle and the *Timaeus*, I propose to draw from the systems of philosophers and seers examples of the relation of their conceptions of the universe, or of God and man, to their more specific thought of the human soul or self. A cosmic system will be in the image of its maker. The conception of man will conform to its general scheme. Conversely, a compelling consciousness of self will affect cosmic thoughts. This is marked in the emotional and wishful thinking of the religious seer seeking to form a responsive scheme of God and the soul. Cosmic systems differ in egocentricity and apparent objectivity. In the objective thought of Plato and Aristotle men's souls are clearly part of the cosmos. The egocentricity of the Indian Upanishads seems to hang the universal absolute around man's absolute self. But views of self and cosmos will always work upon each other. Neither is fully independent.

The factor of choice is present in the construction of both cosmos and self. It has already proved itself in fixing upon these objects of thought, and continues to operate through the mind's adhering to them instead of wandering to other things. In the construction of the self it lays stress on qualities regarded as best. Less obviously, and yet persistently, choice affects the structure of the cosmos, or at least the power moving it. What is it that approves and chooses? A complete answer might solve the problem of the self. Crudely speaking, the approving and choosing agent seems to be a comprehensive self-consciousness of *me* and the world, or rather of me-in-the-world. Such a self-consciousness should select the most broadly coördinating elements of life and being.

Approval and choice inhered in Plato's thinking. His thoughts of man as well as of the cosmos issued from his conviction of the primordial reality and creative power of mind. It was mind that from the chaos of matter first created the cosmos, which is order. As order and as the creation of mind the cosmos is both spiritual and real. It is an unfailing creative process possessed of power. Through it human souls were formed and provided with bodies as materials upon which the spiritual order works. Bodies are powerless in themselves and have only derivative reality and truth. The creator was good and sought to make the cosmos good. But the cosmos was incapable of perfection because of its physical elements. The cosmos or created soul of the world could not completely triumph over material recalcitrancy, which is ἀνάγκη. Likewise human souls, set in bodies, cannot completely triumph over the lusts in which they are entangled, at least while the connection lasts.

The soul of the world is not sheer mind or reason; nor is the soul of man. Love and desire — eros — are of the nature of both. Human souls have feelings, impulses, and desires which, though partly impelled by the body, are capable of being tempered and infused with the higher qualities of mind and reason. Issuing from the cosmic process, the soul shares its total psychic nature. Eros may be the chief mover of the soul's activities; it is the principle of selective striving, which brings out the soul's nobler faculties, and clears them of temporal dross.

The soul's goodness lies in maintaining the supremacy of its attributes of mind and reason, through which it shares in the truth and reality of the cosmos.[1] This is at once its choice of the best and its cosmic reconcilement. The soul's entangled qualities are not to be expunged or nullified, any more than ἀνάγκη can be eliminated from the cosmos. To keep them in proper subjection is the soul's discipline. Its best faculty is broad and instructed wisdom which will consider all elements of human life. There can be no higher wisdom than to know oneself, as the Oracle commands.[2] The directing power of the cosmos is not unfeeling nor unmindful of righteous men here and hereafter. Whatever befalls them works for their good, and further happiness awaits them after the soul's separation from the body whereby it may reach a better knowledge of goodness and truth.[3] The soul is immortal so far as it shares in eternal spiritual realities.

Plato's psychology is no more egocentric than his whole philosophy. His soul's immortality could not be the supreme end with one so taken with the power of universal

[1] Obvious analogies illustrate the kinship between man and the cosmos. The virtues of individual and city are the same. Justice and temperance consist in the due functioning of the qualities both of individuals and groups, and reflect the order of the cosmos wherein no element shall overstep its bounds. Analogies between human conduct and world processes were current with Plato's predecessors.

[2] *Phaedrus*, 229 E.

[3] *Republic*, 613 A and 614 A ff.

spiritual validities. Moreover it fell in with his philosophy and the universal quality of the elements making up the human soul that Plato attempted no definition of that utter paradox which combined the dialectic dilemmas of each and all its parts. Had any dialogue ever unraveled its particular dialectic puzzle? But Plato left no doubt of what he knew the Self was not, making it clear in Socrates' reply to Crito's question, "In what way shall we bury you?"

"In any way you like: but you must get hold of me, and take care that I do not run away from you."

"Then he turned to us and added with a smile: 'I cannot make Crito believe that I am the same Socrates who have been talking and conducting the argument; he fancies I am the other Socrates whom he will soon see a dead body — and he asks how shall he bury me? And though I have spoken many words in the endeavour to show that when I have drunk the poison I shall leave you and go to the joys of the blessed.'"

Although emphasizing the more disentangled and completely spiritual attributes of the soul, Plato did not shut out the violent impulses of bodily passion. Stoicism, however, especially in its first strenuousness, was more exclusive. Zeno and Chrysippus found in reason not merely the soul's highest quality but its essential nature. This conviction springing from predilection and accordant choice was a moving factor in the Stoic scheme of the universe and man. The chief Stoical interest was ethics, centered upon man's attainment of his good, which lay in contentment and an unshakeable peace of mind based upon reason. Only that can be a good which accords with his essentially reasoning nature. But human reason is part of the divine reason constituting universal law. Hence only that can be a good for man which flows from his reason acting in harmony with the divine reason of the universe. The will so to act is virtue, man's chief if not sole good. Herein is his contentment and refuge against life's storms as well as lures, which make up the motley mass of things indifferent to the Stoic sage.

Stoicism passed on from the austerities of Zeno through the eager reasonings of Chrysippus and the devoutness of Cleanthes. It had laid aside much of its logical priggishness before entering the virile atmosphere of Rome, there to become the pillar of republican virtue and liberty. Bodily health and innocent enjoyments were accepted as conditional goods; social duties were recognized, and, touched with the cosmopolitanism of the time, Stoicism asserted the common brotherhood of man. Yet its reasonings upheld its central conviction that man's veritable nature is one with his beatitude, set in a virtuous will which knows itself part of the righteous will and law of God. The Stoic soul was a choice and a struggle to attain the chosen state, like the Platonic, but with more positive rejection of all else.

For convenience I have spoken of Stoicism before turning to Aristotle's comprehensive biological treatment of souls, or grouped attributes, of man. In his scheme plants, animals, and men show successive groups of activities called "souls," distinguished as nutritive, sensitive, and intellectual or rational. The nutritive is common to all organisms; the sensitive belongs to animals, the rational to man alone. Thus the more general underlies that which has emerged more specifically. Aristotle perceived a continuous progression from the scant life of the lowest plants to those living more abundantly, such as are almost animals; and so on through the sense-life of animals to the full sensitive and rational life of man.

Have these souls attributes unshared by matter? For the nutritive and sensitive soul the answer is in the negative, since matter is the material of their actions. Yet they have an end or form; — of their own? A living body is a body with a soul, which is its form in Aristotelian phrase. Thus the soul or souls may be the realization or actuality (as contrasted with potentiality) of the body — its ἐντελέχεια. At least this is true of the nutritive and sensitive souls. But that soul, or mental attribute, which is thought is not a form of the body, and may exist independently of matter. Dividing reason into passive and active, he finds in the former the material images of thought. These are used by the active reason, which is an actuality independent of matter and capable of surviving the body's dissolution — at least, according to some statements of the Master.

Souls with Aristotle seem to represent the achieved form and actuality of human nature. His broadly biological discussion moves on from the organic life of plants and animals to the activities of man. There is no break, unless the active reason be taken as different from the rest. At all events, trailing a grand breadth of consideration, Aristotle's thought of the soul, or human nature actualized, establishes reason as the supreme attribute. His scheme by no means lacks the quality of choice.

II

Aristotle's psychology has affinity with the modern sciences dealing with organisms. He would have accepted evolution, though perhaps with some logical catchings of the breath. And how sympathetically other Greeks would have regarded evolution is suggested by the saying of Anaximander (however he meant it) that man was something like a fish in the beginning. So it is again convenient to disregard chronology and see how the psyche fares in the evolutionary view of organic nature. Biologists accept evolution though uncertain as to its method or nature. That a temporal succession of organisms has come into existence on the earth is proved by the field sciences of geology and paleontology. Another kind of investigation offers suggestions of vestigial recapitulation of ancestral forms in the embryos of later species. As to how evolution works, there is the well-buttressed theory of natural selection, taken in connection with the effect of environment on all organisms and the universal fact that members of every species differ within certain limits. From the laboratory genetics gives its evidence of variations in the genes causing modifications in the adult.

There is considerable evidence as to the general courses

by which plants and animals have reached their present physical and psychical efficiency. The psychic elements are at first so rudimentary and difficult to trace that attention is held perforce by the succession of forms adapted to the better exercise of physical energy. But through the tertiary period, say from the advent of mammals, the growth of brain becomes of manifest importance for the animal's welfare. Bodily strength and efficiency are needed, but it is rather their purposeful direction by the brain and nervous system that seems to quicken evolution.

Growth of brain has been the physical accompaniment of the advance in intelligence and emotional sensitiveness from apes to man. There has been no increase in strength or general agility, but a serviceable development of the hand and sensory system. Looking into the contents of man's psychic nature and consciousness, we find them marvelously cumulative. No element of the mammalian character has been lost. There is still the full round of appetite, lust, proneness to rage and passion. But a higher level of feeling has been added, connected with perception and memory and touched with intelligence. So we rise to the mental and rational traits in which other animals have but rudimentary share. Informed by feeling and sense perception, they fulfill their office of discrimination with varying effectiveness and bring some order to the *omnium gatherum* of the human psyche. Consciousness becomes a realization of self and the contrasted outer world, and seems to be the medium of this rational ordering. There may result a chosen self, which recognizes and accepts the rule of reason and perceives the value of beneficent social impulses. The self may be moulded and fashioned by the man's total coördinated experience and wisdom.

Evolution contains no principle pointing to a self or soul or mind capable of living after the body ceases to function. It cannot see beyond the dissolution and re-combination of elements no longer working as an organism. Knowing nothing of a God at the beginning, it finds no basis for an immortal mind or soul emerging from the human end of the process. Every historical conception of self has emerged from a consonant view of the cosmos. An immortal soul needs a God or an Absolute behind it, as will appear in the contrast between the Brahmanism of the Upanishads and Buddhism, the rebel child. Holding to a universal Absolute, Brahmanism saw in man a cor-relative Absolute, the Atman; but Buddhism rejected both together.

III

Plato rejected no element that might be brought to subordination in the human soul, and Aristotle welcomed them all to his biological kingdom as evolution does to-day. Quite different are those partly religious systems which reject much of the world and human nature as dangerous or actually evil. Yet they have this in common with the rest, that the conception of man always falls in with their scheme of the world and God.

The degree of interest taken in the cosmos and its phe-nomena suggests a general line of cleavage. Where these matters are objects of keen intellectual curiosity, as with the Greeks, the world is an object of supreme interest, and every element of human nature is recognized. There is no implication that the passionate animal impulses are evil, since they are part of the scheme and may be ordered and made use of. On the other hand, slight intellectual interest in the surrounding world leads to a disparagement of natural phenomena and disapproval of the human qualities that are stirred by things of sense. This is shown in the history of Indian thought. Again, though the early Christians had no dislike for things of sense, they had won such hold on life eternal that this world's affairs no longer signified. The present life was but a sojourning — παροικία; and as temporal entanglements were apt to divert the soul from its true aim, they were dangerous and evil. It was safer to renounce the world. To become a monk or anchorite was a logical course for men and women who clung to eternal life and a God of punishment as well as love, in whom was anchored their salvation.

In Brahmanism and Buddhism the principle of world-renunciation was rooted in temperamental and philosophical aversion rather than in any looked-for eternal life. To the Indian temper life seemed a round of pain and suffering, carried on remorselessly by the ever-recurring death entailed by accepted doctrines of transmigration. Emancipation from rebirth was the goal of both systems. In Brahmanism the Absolute and the Self united with it were attainable by cessation from desire: "He who is without desire is himself his own desire — he is Brahman."

For the emancipated sage there is after death no consciousness, with its restless notions of duality.

Buddhism, although a metaphysical and psychological revolution, seems to us westerners to follow the same path to the same goal. There is no Absolute and no substantial and enduring self, but only causation and consequence. From knowledge of this principle and the realization that all individual life is suffering, Gotama was loosed from the craving which is sorrow and entails rebirth. He thus became the Buddha. Ignorance is the cause of human misery; knowledge brings deliverance. Through the complete destruction of desire no soul is released, for none existed; but a painful chain of causation is severed. Love and devotion to the Buddha made this pitiless system a religion. Brahmanism, in accordance with its principles, constructed an absolute human self; Buddhism in accordance with its principles, made a selfless self — an unsubstantial eddy in causation's stream.

IV

The Christian Gospel held no metaphysics. It was altogether a religion; its single theme was man's relationship to God. Jesus' life was held in his relationship to the Father. Human relations and duties likewise find their source in the relationship of all believers to God: "Ye are sons of a Father and therefore brethren." *Creator omnium* is indeed the Christian God. More intimately He is a Father to his children, with all the support and love and care implied. The Christian soul[4] exists substantially; but it is held in the divine relationship; its life consists in fulfillment of its relationship to God. Such seems the kernel of the utterances of the two most creative minds of the apostolic and patristic church, Paul and Augustine. With Paul the relationship is fervently in and through Christ. Augustine realizes that only through "the mediator of God and men, the man Christ Jesus" can man reach that thought and love of God which saves.[5] But he is more apt than Paul to turn directly *ad Deum* whose will it is that the Christian soul should seek him. "Fecisti nos ad te et inquietum est cor nostrum donec requiescat in te" are the most frequently quoted words of any Christian saint, unless perhaps the other clinching statement: "Deum et animam scire cupio. Nihil ne plus? Nihil omnino."[6]

However much the mind may follow inborn tendencies, whatever makes the constant topic of its thought affects the manner and points the direction of its growth. A dominant group of convictions and interests persisting through generations will produce minds of definite character. Such was the effect of the Christian faith. Through its passionate conceptions of God and the soul, it created qualities, even faculties, in believers. Its formative influence can be traced from its first Gospel fervor, on through dogmatic constructions, till it becomes the moving energy of Augustine's emotionalized intellectual genius; then onward to its spiritual ordering of society and the heights of

[4] I use the word "soul" loosely, without attempting a definition.
[5] *De civitate Dei* xi. 2.
[6] *Confessions* i. 1. 1.

its expressional power in the Middle Ages. Conversely, the Faith reached a fuller round of application and gained in human feeling through the action of faculties responding to its influence. One may distinguish intellectual and emotional phases without underrating their constant effect upon each other and their frequently united action.

Since acceptable rational statement was a first necessity in a world of quick-witted pagans, the early Fathers through fierce disputes and violent disclaimers pressed on to an articulate formulation of the Faith substantially in current terms of Hellenistic philosophy and Roman law. Thus the Nicene creed was made, buttressed upon rational supports and the efficient organization of the Catholic Church, the sole vehicle of true and saving belief. Dogmatic formulation and the Church suited men's minds and tended to fix them in a certain groove. The Middle Ages appropriated and mastered the patristic formulation and made it into a comprehensive system which took final form in the *Summa theologiae* of Aquinas. Constant occupation with theology moulded the medieval intellect, which was little interested in the natural world.

The emotional growth of the Christian soul conformed to its understanding of the Faith. The poles were love and fear: the love of God and Christ and Mary; the fear of hell, with anxious misgivings as to the world. The medieval mind clung to the suffering Christ and Mary's interceding pity which saved so many souls from her Son's righteous condemnation in the Day of Judgment. It was obsessed with a fear which harked back to the Saviour's denunciations and drew added horror from writings of Pope Gregory the Great. This terror wormed itself into the nooks and crannies of daily life. Often smothered by the brute violence of men, it struck back in times of defeat and drove the wretch to grovel in ashes in the hour of death. Fear of the world, often intensifying to hatred, was its creature.

In varying degrees the intellectual faculty of reason promoted the energy and expression of Christian emotion. This gathers to a torrent in St. Bernard. His passionate nature was focussed in his love of God and hatred of whatever threatened a soul's salvation. His hatred is as fierce as his love is ardent, tender, pitying. Both give voice in utterances reaching rhythms of passion. Yet he sets forth the love of God rationally and shows why man should love Him without stint or measure. Well reasoned is his fervent exposition of the four stages of that love which in the fleshly creature begins with self-love. Then, seeing that he cannot live of himself, man begins to love God, but only for his own sake. Tasting of God's sweetness, he begins to love Him for Himself, and finally God alone is loved and man loves himself only for God's sake. Good grounds are given for each stage of the soul's devotion. Bernard's love of Jesus is more personal and quivering, and yet is ever passing from love of the Christ-man to love of the Christ-god.[7]

It was different with Francis of Assisi. He was not a

[7] See, on St. Bernard, ch. xviii of *The Mediaeval Mind*.

reasoning being. Sheer love made him an incarnation of the Christ-life upon earth. He was *filled* with the love of Jesus; and as Jesus loved all men, so did Francis, and all God's creatures too, even such elements as fire and water, calling them brothers. Rancor and hatred found no place in one who did not hate even heretics or the prelates who set themselves against the utter love which was Christ's gospel. He approached them through love of *sancta obedientia* and the humility of Jesus. He was not learned nor a theologian, but a joyful lover always. Joy and love inspired and peopled his imagination. It would be hard to deny that Francis' soul was made and fashioned by the love of God.

V

Love of God inspired the passionate thought and yearning of the Christian *vita contemplativa*. Quite as moving was the fear of hell that prompted the rejection of the world, and the temper which abhorred its lusts or intellectually despised them. The former is exemplified in St. Peter Damiani, who in eleventh century Italy would gladly have lived the hermit life with its passionate rejections, its austerities and flagellations, and its joy in the "gift of tears" crowning the hermit's love of God and sense of his own vileness. Damiani's writings are outcries against the reeking corruption of clergy and laity alike. Alas! Pope Hildebrand kept dragging him through it, to his sorrow and the peril of his soul. Well he knew that "whoever would reach perfection should keep within the cloister of his seclusion, cherish spiritual leisure and shudder at traversing the world as if he were about to plunge into a sea of blood. For the world is so filthy with vices that any holy mind is befouled even by thinking about it." More tolerantly, he can admit that "many are the ways to God, but among them is no path so sure, so free from obstacles [as the hermit life] . . . which eliminates occasions for sin and cultivates the virtues pleasing to God." [8]

Fear of the world and desire to perfect the soul for eternity sent many a layman and many a distinguished churchman to seek peace and salvation in monastic seclusion. Such a churchman was Bruno, founder of the Carthusian order of hermit monks in the year 1084. In the next generation the "Meditations" of Guigo, its fifth prior, are a supreme expression of remorseless logic and intellectual contempt for the world. "Easy is the way to God," says Guigo, "since it advances by laying off burdens. . . . Thou hast been clinging to one syllable of a great song and art troubled when that wisest singer proceeds in His singing. For the syllable which alone thou wast loving is withdrawn from thee, and others succeed in order. He does not sing to thee alone, nor to thy will, but His." [9]

In these brief instances religious emotion may be dis-

---

[8] Cf. *The Mediaeval Mind*, ch. XVII and ch. XI, 4, on Damiani. Though drawn from solitude himself, he found solace in writing the *Vita* of Romuald, founder of Camaldoli, who was permitted to lead a complete life of austerities, extreme and picturesque to read of.

[9] The *Meditationes* of Guigo are in Migne's *Patrologia Latina*, vol. 155, col. 601–631. They have always seemed to me of great beauty. I have translated a number of them in *The Mediaeval Mind*, vol. I, ch. XVII.

tinguished from the intellectual appropriation of the
Faith. Yet the two join in the supreme creations of the
medieval genius — the structure and ornamentation of
cathedrals and the form and contents of the *Divina Commedia*. Their scholastic union is sanctioned by the major
arguments of Aquinas' *Summa theologiae*, which do not
fail to recognize the office of the Christian emotions in
the Faith that saved through the heart's devotion as well
as the mind's enlightenment.

The system of Thomas is whole and complete, embracing God and the human soul with the rest of the creature
world. God is perfect being and the supreme good, immaterial, eternal, infinite. In Him are the prototypal
forms of all things. Creation is an emanation or going
out from this universal exemplar and cause. The soul is
incorporeal and incorruptible, unmixed with body and
yet the body's form and consummation. While in the
body the soul has appetites and desires inclining it to
what it perceives through the bodily senses and to
what it knows through the intellect. The irascible and
concupiscent appetites make up the former inclination,
while the latter acts through rational knowledge as discriminating and determining will. Working through its
selection of ways and means and secondary goods, the
will directs itself toward the soul's final end, which is
beatitude.

God loves all existences passionlessly, and in one and
the same act of will; but as His love creates goodness,
He may be said to love the better things the more. Man's

love does not create goodness, but is drawn by it. All is from God, and that which seems most freely bestowed is grace, the divine influence disposing the intelligence and will toward good. Faith comes through grace and is formed and completed in *Caritas* — *fides formata*. The perfection of man's intellectual nature is not simply knowing, but must be joined to the will directed toward God in *Caritas*. Perfect beatitude rests on both love and knowledge.

VI

A number of instances from Greece, India, and the Christian Middle Ages have been given of somewhat anthropomorphic cosmologies and conceptions formed analogously of a human self or soul. Approval and choice affected these constructions of the wishful mind. A more difficult task would be to trace like influences and connections in modern philosophies and religious thinking. I am unequal to it. The cosmos has become an essentially boundless universe. The agency of choice and approval is obscure, and the analogy with human nature has vanished. Today man's self or soul not merely resists analysis as of old but tends to disintegrate into process and behavior. This seems true in science and philosophy. In religious belief a soul still lurks, with its immortality slipping from it.

So I abandon the cosmic end of my comparison, and no more than heretofore do I propose any direct assault upon the problem of the self. I mean to follow a trail which will

be of my own stepping, and yet one possibly pointed to
by the intellectual tendencies of our time. You cannot lift
yourself out of the ocean by your bootstraps nor disen-
tangle your mind from current thought. None can escape
today from the mental meshes of process and evolution.
Nothing is isolated or in and of itself alone. Everything
rises from an infinitude of antecedents and concomitants.
There is no sudden event or newly formed creation. Yet
there is continual innovation. No present repeats its past.
An immanent creativity, or energy of change, works in
the inorganic masses of earth, sun, and universe. Perhaps
those masses may be just energy. In organisms energy has
become what we call life, finding it more pointed and
articulate than the energy of the rocks. In the geologic
series of evolving forms the passing members evidently
were alive, which may not justify our saying that the evolutionary process is alive. There seems an infinitude of
factors; yet in their operation some of us recognize a
purpose. At all events the evolutionary process has its
pointings. For the later organisms possess faculties not
appearing in the earlier and exhibit a greater range of
conduct.

There are three major impulses in plants and animals, —
feeding, propagation, and an instinctive avoidance of injury and pursuit of a favorable environment. These may
be placed under some general principle of organic action
like that of urge and relief. The universal drive for food is
obvious. Propagation appears as the natural end and often
final act of plants and many animals. A plant follows these

two modes of urge and relief mercilessly, and so do animals for the most part. One may not impute rage and violence to the lowest animal forms; but such excitements are evident in insects and prominent features of the behavior of birds and mammals, including man. The third organic impulse or mode of urge and relief seems coextensive with the total behavior of the organism and parallels the complex range of its life. It culminates in the manifold and irrepressible greed and violence of men.

The new creature emerging from the process of conception carries the rudiments of its later faculties and apparently some principle making for their common action. Its cells begin to work as parts of an organism whose integral wholeness consists in their coöperation, which is of the essence of organic life and its first mystery. Under the constraint of being together the cells constitute a field of action for each other. The least impeded conduct for a cell is to act with reference to the rest; this is to act as part of an organism. The larger bodily organs likewise have functional efficiency only as coöperating parts. Since they do act as parts of a whole, even to the extent of making good the shortcomings of each other, every functional activity seems, at least in man, to involve the entire psycho-bodily organism. For no psychic action is isolated and independent any more than a bodily function.

The principle of urge and relief passes on (even from such low bodily acts as defecation) into mental activity, and becomes motive and expression or fulfillment. Conversely, feeling and thought may turn to speech or vocal noises. If thought or feeling be logically prior, there is often immediacy of effect. Probably no single motive or functional impulse prompts birds to sing or squawk, dogs to bark or whine, lions to roar and growl, or men to burst into cries or articulate utterance. Such expressions intensify feeling and may clarify the thought or motive which takes form through expression, as in literature and art. In these ways the organism grows, consciousness and thought advance, selfhood asserts itself. The growth of the human individual has clearer continuity than the evolution of its presumptive precursors. But the principle of urge and relief can hardly be excluded from either process.

Analogy between the cosmos and the self is hard to trace in modern thought. Yet choice still affects conceptions of the self. Choice and the restraint of opposing impulses tend to evoke a standard, which is the self. The next step may be the approval of distinctive human traits — the mental faculties and the feelings and impulses moving them. Thoughts of an ideal may come, with endeavor for its realization, which is the felicity of human nature at its highest.

But what is anything and how can anything be except in its relationships? — again a teaching of modern thought. The human personality cannot develop fully in itself alone, but only through its relations and adjustments with what is not itself. Self-fulfillment for the human creature lies in physiological and mental harmony within and in unison of action with its environment and finally with God. The motive of unity with the divine extends the man's purpose to a complete universality of regard, which readily turns to love, the builder of the self and of its world.

VII

The salient features of ancient systems emerge in the perspective of history. We have no such aid for the whirl of thought about us. No soldier in the thick of fight sees the battle. But he is part of it, and I am part of the spiritual maze in which I live. I know something of the morsel which is me and remember its experience. My experience, my growth, seems to have kept itself individual and even disengaged from the masses contributing to it.

I am impressed by the continuousness, even the unity of my life, and find nothing incongruous in its successive stages from youth to age. The elements of myself seem always to have been there. I am inclined to accept the general truthfulness of memory, although later years reshape earlier impressions. Definite incidents may verify the feelings of childhood. While riding with my father in a horse-car the recollection of an afternoon fishing with him in the Harlem River started my tears, for it brought the thought of a future when he would be dead. My passionate love for him returns to me now tinged with remorse for later inconsiderate conduct when I was absorbed in my own plans. But I was a loving child, and the faculty of loving has not left me. Such states of feeling can be separated from the mental interests of boyhood, early stages of an intellectual curiosity which is still mine. And yet, from childhood on, feeling and thought went hand in hand.

Qualities of human nature individualized in me became my growing self. Growth carries the conflicts of selfhood. In part I formed myself through choice, choosing what I would be; and my choice and formative thought of self accorded with my idea of the cosmos in its efficient nature, which I take to be the purpose and will of God of which the cosmos is the exemplification. Herein I find analogy between cosmos and self; and herein too I seek my ultimate adjustment as well as the final unity of my own self. For that lies in the union of purpose with purpose, the individual's with the universal and divine.

It is no simple matter to trace one's composite progress, which presents development of faculty with an emerging choice of approved qualities. Perhaps one is always making decisions and acting upon them. They enter all human conduct, whether impulsive, suggested and constrained, or apparently volitional. But I can look back on what still seem to me three cardinal decisions and consequent action, all three involving wish, consideration, and choice — choice of what I saw would affect my later life.

The first was made when I was barely fifteen. Tiring of schoolbooks and school, I flung out and took a place as errand boy in a ship-broker's office. Soon getting enough of that, I went west with my father and extracted a position from a mining company in a crude Nevada town. Here was decision and action boyishly accepted as determining my career. Many motives entered; a hankering for novelty and adventure blended with raw and ignorant consideration. It was a blowing off of steam and cleared the atmosphere. I still read books, and after a few months began to question the wisdom of my conduct. I saw that the rough Nevada life was not for me, and decided to return east, go to Harvard, and become an educated man suited for some high role. Though I was not yet seventeen, this second decision represented a better judgment of myself.

The third, toward which the second may have pointed, proved to be a final abandonment of the world of affairs for a life of thought and study — the *vita activa* was exchanged for the *vita contemplativa*. This decision was not reached in college nor till I had studied law, tried out the practice, and written a law book. I turned to the limitless and joyful task of tracing in history the manifold ways of thought and emotion and related endeavor. It became the wellspring of my maturing self. I drew from it emotional as well as intellectual growth, and gained from the same manifold task a principle of choice as to what should be approved. In this pursuit I found exhaustless stores of feeling and desire, of judgments, standards, and motives which instructed and formed my mind and in some measure became part of myself.

Knowledge is the web to be filled and colored with feeling and desire. Looking back to the curiosities and perceptions of boyhood's years, I recall my capture by phrenology. A shop was given to it on Broadway, where I bought a plaster head showing all the bumps. Church hours were beguiled by the study of bald heads around me. I was always a reader, and afterwards at Harvard learned much from books and academic courses. More strenuous discipline came from study of the law and constant trying out of legal thought, especially from composing a treatise on corporations.

Passing from the law into wider avenues of thought and endeavor, I won infinite instruction and a larger view. I studied the achievement of each people sympathetically, fascinated by the efforts of men to bring their lives into harmony with their convictions. In every instance, it seemed to me, something was won of truth and general value. Ancient China with its great Confucius presented enduring social verities. Indian thought plumbed the depths of sorrow-stricken transience. But in the bright light of Greece what did I not learn of glorious acts and strivings, of shifting civic governments, and the often futile plans of men to curb their own violence? The very course of Greek philosophy taught me much even when declining from speculation to utility in Stoicism. The last sets one on the road to Rome, practical-minded, legal, an imperial civilizer. If there was intellectual shrinkage, the ageing world showed broadening of feeling and sympathy even such as came to my own rather individual self.

Although fear of the gods and a felt kinship with them touched every phase of Greek and Roman life, religion was later to assume a new and masterful dominance. The source was the person and teaching of Jesus with its passionate background of prophet and psalmist. A new and measureless emotion swept the receptive pagan world, which on its side sought to extend and rationalize what it was about to accept. So grew the dogmatic faith that was destined to move the Middle Ages with the love of God and fear of hell. It entered my nature too.

The centuries following the Middle Ages opened their riches to my mind. Omitting this further tale, I will try to suggest under the symbol of love how this heightened knowledge, feeling, desire, and will became part of me. I think love in its many modes is the great builder of self. Its simpler forms moved my childhood — above all, love of my father so intense as to bring anxiety for his safety when he was out of my sight; a love which carried the belief that no other child had such parents as mine. This assumption leavened my childhood; it would have poisoned my nature to have thought ill of them. No need to add that approval entered my child's love for a little playmate of the opposite sex.

Such were the loves of childhood. Through all the years of youth and manhood on to old age, there was no time when I did not revere some girl or woman, with a love belonging to my total mind. I was never swept by thoughtless passion, if passion ever is quite thoughtless. Love has been with me a teacher of the mind, or rather part of all the mental faculties. It could not but include desire of the other's good, a desire that becomes utter tenderness with the years.

Opinions and beliefs, however intellectualized, are wishful. Their reach and character hang on the nature of the individual. A youth's attitude toward life does not spring either from logic or intuition. It is a synthesis and symbol of himself and his experience, changing only as he changes and thus is more stable than his particular opinions or beliefs. A religious nature that naturally turns toward God is apt, barring catastrophes, to continue to the end. At least this has been so with me. Brought up in current beliefs, I soon fell out with them. I did not shift to unbelief but turned to more generalized modes of religious thought and feeling. I have remained trustful, acceptant of a divine purpose, and can still confirm what I wrote when I was twenty-six: " 'Tis the mighty complex frame of things I love, and in the contemplation of which I find peace. . . . I go under — what of that? God still purposes, and there shall be some final good."

This was written when hope had faded of winning the desire of my heart. I am grateful that no experience, however grievous, ever enraged or embittered a life that has throughout been happy with a happiness assured. I have been enabled to accept lovingly whatever came, as from the hand of the great giver. Love and a loving recognition of a divine purpose influenced my study and understanding of the tale of human endeavor. Plato in another way discloses love's power to uplift the mind, less explicitly in its demiurgic role in the *Timaeus* than in Socrates' discourse on the love of beauty in the *Symposium*. The movement is from the concrete to the universal: — A youthful lover observes beautiful forms, falls in love with one of them, and creates beautiful thoughts from his passion.

Perceiving the kinship between the beauty of one and the beauty of another, he sees that bodily beauty is everywhere the same, and will not love a single body excessively but become a lover of all beautiful forms. He next perceives a nobler beauty in souls than in bodies, and will know the beauty of laws and institutions and sciences, and realize the kinship of beauty in them all. He will create beautiful thoughts in love of wisdom and, seeing all in due order, will at last discern that wondrous beauty which is everlasting and neither waxes nor wanes, nor is fair in one respect and foul in another, but is beauty absolute in which all perishing beauties share.

Love of beauty is desire reaching ever toward that which is more universal. The Platonic goal of absolute beauty is difficult for us, and a Greek proverb said, as well as Plato and Spinoza, that beauty is hard to grasp. To me all beauty is moving and dynamic, and I would translate absolute beauty (Plato might not disagree) into purpose — the divine purpose. This I can love and partly understand. The thought of purpose comes to me also from the course of evolution, — even from the reluctant testimony of natural science.

In conclusion, returning to the three major decisions already spoken of and what came of them, I seem to have exceeded the lot of most men in the free choice of a course of life which was to be happily followed. Yet no implication is intended that the decision was entirely my own. If I recognize a cosmic purpose, more intimate and sure is my conviction of some guidance in those devotions and endeavors which contributed to the making of myself. Love of a divine purpose — universal but also individually directed — is my faith and now in sorrow brings me peace. Through this love thought and feeling are expanded to the limit of a finite nature seeking to realize and fulfill itself to the utmost reaches of its finitude. Carrying on this wishful thinking, life in the body becomes rational and satisfying as preparation but not as culmination. The chosen self will somehow look beyond the terminus of mortal breath.

IV

SOUL OF ARCHILOCHUS

IV

Soul of Archilochus[1]

I

ON PAROS, island of the gleaming rock, my eyes first caught the light of Helios. Fathered by an impetuous man, my mother a slave, childhood with me was passionate and my youth a storm. Our city's walls held more hate than love. Breaking away from some fierce dispute, an angry clique might take ship and look for a new home. I, long called a maligner, would speak truth. Our men were united against foes. In peace common prejudices and like pursuits fostered a working fellowship. There was comradeship among those of us who had shared danger together. Strong impulse as well as ingenious thought marked our Ionian towns. Life was eager with each man and with the people when assembled in the market place.

My own life, now mirrored in memory, is no longer distracted as when in the flesh. It was cast on circumstance. I recall its rancors and can measure its violence. I can still laugh, as once I jested, at my shield thrown away in flight — a deadly shame in Sparta, where they drove me out

[1] An Ionian Greek poet living in the first half of the seventh century before Christ. The ancients placed him next to Homer. Only casual fragments of his poems remain. They deeply influenced Greek poetry and drama.

with jeers. No shame was felt by one who chose to live, knowing how to lose as well as win and raise his head again above the waves. My nature is put best in those iambics spoken to my soul: "Soul, soul! stricken with overwhelming troubles, bear up! Thrust back the onslaught and the ambushed danger, breast to foe. And neither, conquering, foolishly exult, nor, conquered, wail and cry. But in joys rejoice and in evils grieve not overmuch. So learn what rhythm holds men."

I could endure as well as another. Speaking from myself, I counseled a friend that for irreparable ills the gods had given the medicine of steadfastness. I fought and hated. My verse tore those who thwarted the fevered eros that was loosening my limbs. Yet throughout the anger and violence of my life consideration knocked at the door. I could praise valor in a foe, and heeded Odysseus' chiding of the old nurse not to exult over the dead. The unforeseen might descend on any man, like the darkening of the sun at noon. But Zeus gave mind and mood to meet what might befall, and toil brought forth things useful for mortals. I knew that Father Zeus beheld men's knavish as well as lawful deeds, and could raise from the black earth those struck down by ills.

The best was that I ever followed, cherished, and increased within me, the Muses' lovely and mighty gift of verse. Knowing and chanting Homer's poems, I was no imitator. Of myself, above all other men, I moulded those quick iambics to pithy form, made them to sting and bite; made them beautiful in their power to tell the passions and the fates of men. The poet Homer spoke from himself, out of his nature. How else could he? Yet his chant was of what all men might wish for or would shun, with no word of his own chequered lot. I had no song of Zeusborn kings. My verse was of myself — voicing my hates and longings, the passions of the men about me, which often touched me sore: men like myself entangled, driven, reaching a brief success. It was myself, my setting, my needs, often my own dire lot, I sang.

Verse brought me renown in life and fame thereafter. That man called Korax, whose spear let out my breath, might not purify himself before the Pythian priestess, swearing that he killed me fairly. As having slain one sacred to the Muses, he was driven out till he should appease my ghost. I am praised by men in the far times to come; in my island city is set my monument, and men are still bidden to pause before one whose fame had flown from the rising to the setting sun.

I am a mind reflecting and absorbing: doing nothing, I experience. The lusting, fighting body, which was part of me, could endure its present, look back regretfully, or ahead, dreading yet hopeful of the future. But now occurrences no longer succeed each other. Thought carries what once had seemed to go before, and points to what shall be disclosed more clearly. Though a temporal sequence may order events which feed my mind, past and future are manifested in each other. It is all actualization, a flowering rather than succession.

The exertions and endeavors, the turmoil, struggle, and

killing that went on through the Ionian islands and coast cities when I was in the body, and the dire times that saw the barbarians enslave our peoples — this complex of struggling or despairing life, the panorama of it all, is in my thought. Alas! there seems always to have been some clever Ionian whose grasping selfishness wrecked the fortunes of his city, and ruined those civic liberties which are a springboard for intellectual achievement. But my thought swells proudly as it turns to the victory of our Athenians over the Persian foe. And what a flowering followed of civic fullness, and art and drama and philosophy. The mind which now is me takes in the far event and sees the measureless import of Athens for mankind.

There is no rancor in me, and scarcely regret for ill fortune; what seems the past opens to me its why and wherefore reassuringly. Reminiscence as well as thought's fair prospect brings a genial expansion of spirit. Genial, I say, because, while violence and sense-riot do not enter, I am interested and often moved. Discrimination brings desire for whatever discloses itself as truth.

There are sequences in the visible world; also in human knowledge. I have been turning to the thoughts of men who were unborn when I was in the flesh. Then the gods were often on my tongue; I have since queried as to the source of things and their ways of action — the causes, so to speak. There is a Milesian who foretold that on a given day a shadow would push across the sun. Such a shadowing, once seen by me, seemed to overtop all other wonders. Is it such a wonder if a man can foretell it? Its cause lies not in my old gods whose action none could guess. This same Milesian says all things come from water, while a friend of his finds a more unlimited and total source. Heat and cold, and the wet and dry things, separate themselves out of this, while living animals are born of moisture and its warm evaporations. This seems to me real thinking and not just accepting what we used to put in poetry and daily speech.

I see that men will answer such questions in many ways, which shall show their progress in thinking. For myself I mark that these Milesian schemes take no account of that which *I am*, θυμός — soul, mind, will, purpose. So their insufficiency appears. Other thinkers offer me other thoughts. A certain sage makes over this basic matter into numbers and their relationships. He applies like thoughts to human conduct, hoping that through them men will learn to adapt their lives to social needs, eschew violence and gain moderation. I am with him here, little as my bodily life conformed. But as yet my own experience does not agree with his idea of souls passing from a dead body to a live one.

This man lives far to the west, where there are others who are showing how insecure is man's reliance on what his eyes and ears and fingers tell him of the world. One must have thinking, thinking to purge such evidence from contradiction and reach a thought of stable and sure being. I too am drawn to realize how little we can trust the quick message of our senses till thought has gone over and over it, and sifted what they have told us.

But what do I hear from Ephesus of still one who denies that there is any stable being to be tested by thought? He thinks nothing abides; indeed that nothing *is*, but only *becomes*. All is ceaseless change and flux. He calls it fire, and sees it kin to the human soul and the rational principle of the Kosmos. Out of this change and strife comes harmony! Dark are his words; but perhaps a new name for his thought comes echoing dimly from the future — process. From still another I hear there is a power outside the whirl; a thing of might: he calls it *νοῦς*, or mind. And still another younger man will solve the dispute between the Ephesian and the western sages, by cutting up matter into an infinitude of infinitesimals moving eternally throughout the void.

II

Surely my mind has grown thinking these pregnant thoughts of younger men. They shall be called philosophers. Yet all wisdom is not with them. I might have known this while still in the rioting body. For I was myself a poet; and I knew the wisdom of the epics; how they fitted life to the ways of things, and the ways of things to life, and called it fate. Fate might be hard, but it had fitness, as it moved along paths made by the man's temper and conduct, bringing him to a terminus not unforeseen. There was wisdom too in that plodding poet of the *Works and Days*, who died before I was born. Surely the poet has his share of wisdom from the Muse. His inspiration may be a glimpse of the divine ordering, and his verse carry a fuller round of life and truth than the reasonings of my good philosophers.

I am thinking of a great choral poet whose songs are sought and well rewarded by the victors in the games. It is given him above other men to show the golden truth of meaning in these triumphs. Magnificent his odes in words and thought, as they sing how men win in the games as in life by the favor of Zeus, themselves not lacking in valor. God and man's hero nature bring him to the goal of fame, immortalizing him in his passing deed. I am stirred by the lyric wisdom of this great Theban, whose city at this time is far from glorious, to his pain.

I am soon to learn a deeper lesson of life's sure retributions — still under Zeus. Fate had been suitable and fit with my first epic teacher. Its justice and righteousness were now to be revealed. From the Attic stage come the words: "It is the impious act that begets its kind: righteous houses are blest with fair children. The ancient Insolence engenders an offspring of insolence in evil men, an avenging dæmon not to be put off."

I hear the complement and crown of this dread principle: for the man not wholly bad, enlightenment follows retribution; from suffering, wisdom. First among men an Athenian makes clear the web of crime and punishment held in an old story: "He is wise who sings in praise of Zeus, Zeus who leads mortals to be wise: whose law it is that suffering shall teach. Mindfulness of past woes drops on the heart in sleep and makes men wise against their will." Those fixed unwritten laws of Zeus — let no man-sprung edict attempt to override them, sings another poet. From this younger man I gain the subtle principle that intent makes the crime; he whose ill deeds were sufferings, rather than acts, may gain acquittance in the end — win through to expiation.

Drawing wisdom from these men, I became sentient and perceptive through their minds. With them I moved through those great days when we fought off Persia and slavery. In these experiences human life became weightier and gained a new significance. The need was more insistent to understand the good and ill of it, the worth of its perceptions; also the reasons of its fateful courses. Insistence upon man himself began to vitalize and humanize the thinking of men I call philosophers. Those who found ultimate being in the atoms tried to draw the principles of human conduct within the atomic whirl; the ideal of knowledge must include the ideal of life. Philosophy turns to the doer and thinker. I seem to discern man the thinker as henceforth the pivot of his thought, though it embrace the world he lives in — immense, fate-driven, or God-created. The unity of man's nature will insist that what is best for man must be at one with what is true. Philosophy becomes a test, a consistency of thought.

A snub-nosed Athenian goes up and down the city streets, pursues men to the nooks and crannies of their business, questioning, arguing on names and words, seeking meanings that will stand sifting. Some men, and I among them, see the foolishness of current talk as well as the pitfalls in the thinking of the old philosophers. We are nearing new heights, and I perceive that the way up is not merely a path but verily a part of whatever height is reached. Now I see that earlier thoughts, and experience from decade to decade enlarging, still work in the conduct of later men, and in later thought become springs of energy and light. I feel around me a careful weighing of conduct, discernment and skill in sculpture, deepened significance in drama and lyric. New verses are sung in music made for them. Music and line and strophe spring from old, still living, forms. My own iambics, bold and new in their time — no one had used them so cunningly before — have made the drama's dialogue, and more. I am part of it all, and men recite my verses still.

And now I listen to the drastic thinking of men moving in our world. Old opinions are sifted, some thrown aside, but more of them given new form and life. Well-thumbed ideas jostle each other and take on a second youth with our philosophers here at Athens, which is my spirit's home. Above them soars, and sometimes gambols, one who dwells in the conviction that the supreme reality is mind. I possess the proof of this in my own enduring life of thought. Yet I marvel at this philosopher as he fuses the thoughts of former men and of some still living in the flesh. He wields the reasoning power of such as upheld the scheme of being, one and absolute. They are perhaps the springs of his own spiritual truths. But his mind holds also the counter-reasons of the keen Ephesian, so destructive of everything except modes of change. Although repugnant, the atomic doctrines are well understood. Fully appreciating the sense-perceptive and relative nature of knowledge, his reason is steadied by its training in analytic definition from the good snub-nosed teacher. He raises his concepts to principles of life; would win through to a grasp of the supreme good as the surest reality. The impulse is love, purged of lust, straining on to beauty absolute and unchanging.

Alas, perhaps, all of these thoughts are not for me. I have heard the wonderful song of the *Phaedrus* which, in language almost beyond words, tells the passion of the soul divinely maddened by its yearning to fly upward to the beauty from which it fell at birth. I have also in the *Symposium* followed this passion from its genesis in lusts, up through the desire for the better, unto the yearning for the best. It loves souls rather than bodies, and seeks the beauty of laws, institutions, sciences, and that broadest knowledge, which is knowledge of the beautiful — the beauty which is not fair in one respect and foul in another, which neither waxes nor wanes, is neither a becoming nor a perishing: beauty absolute in which perishing beauties share without affecting it.

This is the ideal beauty, or the beauty of the ideal. All reverence for the soaring thought that has conceived and reached it. But I am still a poet and my thought of beauty lives and moves in poetry, in all art, if one will. In beauty, as I think it, there is $\delta\acute{v}\nu\alpha\mu\iota\varsigma$, which is power; and $\delta\acute{v}\nu\alpha\mu\iota\varsigma$ is always in action. A mighty thinker, pupil of this high philosopher, opens his talk on Poetry with the words,

"Let us speak of poetry and its kinds and the δύναμιν of each." He discusses the excellence of poetry, the drama especially. Such excellence falls in with the methods of the poets and the best forms of conduct. Without using the word "beauty," he discloses the qualities of tragedy so as to make clear what is its ideal excellence. My great Theban poet had shown the beauty of the success won by noble striving. Looking further back, I recall the dynamic modes of beauty in the Trojan epic. Helen is most fair to look on and her words are beautiful; but her beauty is not unmoving and her words speak thought that moves so fitly. My great Athenian would agree that fitness, temperance, and the golden mean of self-control are elements of beauty; and one must ascribe the quality of power to his changeless beauty, even as this quality is held in the Unmoved Mover, the conception of his pupil.

Such thoughts as mine concerning beauty find form and life in the supreme trilogy of the master of tragedy. The story of Agamemnon is in everyone's memory. That is the μῦθος, by some called the plot, of the tragedy. It forms and controls the drama. Each incident is held to the measure of its contribution to the action. The personages act and speak in and for the drama. They are sheer agents. Every line they speak reflects the situation and is portentous of what must come. The roots and causes of the tragedy are given in veiled allusion and forebodings understood by all of us. This drama is not invented or composed by the dramatist, but is *revealed* by him in its causal setting to show how it came to pass. In the energy of its language and the suggestions of its images, in the fitness and right functioning of every incident, the play called *Agamemnon* possesses the excellence of power — δύναμις — and so is beautiful. Its beauty is manifested in its dynamic being and the action of its qualities. I find the same beauty in the second play of the trilogy, which brings the over-vengeful murderous queen to her fit and proper death. The third play frees Orestes from the horrors of matricide by proving that his deed was guiltless under the prompting and promise of the gods.

This trilogy may justify my halting criticism of the Athenian philosopher. Doubtless our minds pass upward, as in his *Symposium*, from lower to higher beauties or conceived excellences or powers (δυνάμεις), and thus may reach perhaps a highest thought of beauty. Still, all beauty is dynamic, an activity working in power. At all events, such seems to me the beauty of art and poetry. The structure of a poem sets its dynamic quality, and meter, rhythm, rhyme, are elements of power. Yet no formula can exhaust the depth and riches of fact — of our perception or experience of anything. The recognition of this throughout the talks of that great Athenian is one of the sure proofs of his greatness. To say that beauty is power does not exhaust our experience of beauty. If this dictum applies to drama or to oratory or to the epic, does it touch our feeling for an acanthus leaf or the significance of any deed or human form? Much remains untold, perhaps ineffable.

III

If an immortal spirit, freed from the rancors of the flesh, could be torn by the anguish of those who are near and dear in mortal kinship, immortality would be intolerable. Yet my sympathies are sadly moved by the long war in which Greeks will not give over destroying each other. From the courses of events I foresaw how internecine rivalry was leading to an insatiable war. My grand Athenians need not have been overthrown had they been prudent. Folly in the people and selfish vanity in those who misled them brought on the fatal Sicilian venture. Alas for temperance lost and self-control!

I foresee no end of wars to come: no end to pseudo-patriotism and valor misdirected, all masking cupidity. Foolish mankind will continue even as I was once. Fighting is in the blood; keen minds do not perceive its futility. Yet people are becoming concerned with feeling, interested in the softer as well as the more violent emotions. Love's passion and its counterpart of hate are displayed in tragic drama. The art of sculpture is sensitized in statues showing human moods and emotions; it has abandoned the old calm.

The age of Macedon's semi-barbarian dominance in Greece is here. Hellenism is no longer free. Neither will it liberate itself through Alexander's conquests, nor in his genial effort to make East and West absorb each other. His overarching might and the warring dynasties succeeding him make Greeks feel their powerlessness. Doubtless they were never quite masters of their destinies; now they are conscious of their impotence. The more thoughtful are trying to establish their souls in a self-determined freedom. Prevailing ways of thinking are looking to the welfare of the man within himself. The impelling mood, if not the constructive thought, of these systems enters into me. Not that I am oppressed by any resistless mortal power, seeing that I am all soul and subject to no assault. Am I free? I feel free and yet am a market for whatever human experience comes to my consciousness. I am most deeply affected by what seems truth.

It may be that I reflect the minds of men in every passing present. But I am also a growing soul, and feel growing pains. I have needs and yearnings for a larger adjustment with the universe than had touched my immaturity. If aforetime I tried to propitiate sundry gods, that is now too casual. I must reach accord with the universal and infinite Godhead. For I need to think within the compass of his power. I would yearn and think and act in accordance with his will. I am no mere thinker, but a yearner too.

So I have nought in common with a certain Epicurus who will have it that the gods take no part in men's affairs. They are contented and supine and deaf to prayer. Let men also keep to the least disturbing pleasures, leaving the rest to pass undesired. Then there is no place for fear. Such thoughts suit godless men who scarcely look beyond comforts alike ignoble whether of the mind or body.

The other system has many reasonings that do not appeal to me; otherwise with its ideals. It sets man's peace, even content and happiness, within the conduct of his will, but views his will as part of universal law. With limping arguments it makes that law divine, to wit the will of God — for men an all-ruling providence. It even looks to God as a helpmate within each soul. So it would turn to Him in prayer, but with slight rational assurance of response.

A sense of human impotence seems to move both these systems. They lack the energy which lifted the thought of the Athenian philosopher to an assured spiritual reality. Not for long will these systems give strength and gladness to their advocates. Even now do they help men widely? If stronger souls can make a fortress of the human will, that is an empty notion for the masses who have little strength and many fears. They need outer aid and comfort, say from the gods and daemons touching whom they are anxious day and night. Men and women are making a careful stepping anent the gods. They see omens everywhere, and watch the turning of a feather to find what fortune or misfortune awaits their acts. More than formerly they seek their fortunes in the inexorable stars. It is all an anxious stepping.

Yet Stoicism, the better one of these two systems, has raised the thought of God. Looking back upon my fellows in the flesh, I recall how all of us feared the gods and would buy their favor by silly acts and gifts. We imagined the gods to be like our own grasping or groveling selves, only secure from mischance. There was too much of man and of the unaccountable ways of nature in our religion. Even Zeus in Homer was far from fixed and righteous, and could be deceived, lured by his own whims or lusts. There was too much of *me*, Archilochus, and too little of the divine in Zeus. Only afterwards Aeschylus made him a righteous dispenser of justice. Probably my own thoughts of God are broader still.

In these many years after Alexander's death we Greeks go here and there among the peoples less disdainfully. Stoicism expresses the new feeling that there is something of the same in men everywhere. It even teaches that all men are brothers — a shaky kinship, as it still seems to me. The rule of Alexander and his successors is being replaced by the power of a great republic in the west, soon to become imperial. If these mighty kingdoms and their supplanter have made men know the individual's impotence, the Empire begins to make its subjects behave as citizens of a world. They are governed by a single ruler and a central ministration of law. There is a state religion, somewhat thin. Under its aegis various religious practices and many curious superstitions minister to the prejudices of races and the wants or weaknesses of men and women. All people borrow religion and rites and superstitions. What is thoughtful blends with the absurd. Religion flourishes through the common need of protection in an all too chancy world. This need reaches out beyond the life of the present body, looking for some ghostly safety for the shade. Hope plots the ways and means of its fulfillment.

Our Greek religion gave scanty aid beyond the funeral pyre, only certain "mysteries" lending a rather particular support. Roman religion has nothing more. So we Greeks and dumbly Hellenized Romans, finding our own cults wanting, are willing to try out assurances from the stocks of other nations. The choice is wide indeed.

IV

A certain restless Jewish people pushes about the world. They are unsocial and uncomfortable, not like other men. They call the rest of the world gentiles, just as we Greeks used to call them all barbarians. They pull back their skirts as from defilement with gentile touch, and yet seek converts for their faith. For religion is a faith with them; there is passion in their relation to their god. I am a Hellene and never cared for Jewish views. They have no thought of natural law; everything hangs on the will of their Jehovah-god. Reading their books, I find his will was frequently violent and cruel. This people was carried captive into Asia, and suffered dire discipline of body and spirit. Their captivity may have brought new thoughts, possibly some notion of a future life and a conviction that they had a mission in the world. It would seem that the sins of the Jews and their calamities inspired their prophets to elevate Jehovah from a jealous God of one small people to a righteous ruler of all the peoples of the earth. He is made a universal god, and yet is still a person with a will and character having no kinship with natural law.

Here was something new for me: that a god should become God universal and supreme and yet continue sheer personality and not a symbol or element or phase of law, into which the Stoic god was always turning. With all his righteousness and might, Jehovah had also love, at least for his own people. Elements of like thoughts had harbored in my own Greek self, but had never formed a convincing personality. It seems to me that personality is needed in a ruler over human destinies and for the purposeful creation of the world.

Renovation and new life for the Jewish faith are emerging out of Judaism itself in its old home of Palestine; no building out of ceremonies, but a flowering of the spirit likely to burst the old bonds of the Jewish law. Righteousness had lain in its strict fulfillment. Now a man arises, a prophet or perhaps more than a prophet, who declares that he comes to fulfill the law, but in a way that destroys its letter. He teaches that righteousness does not lie in doing or refraining, but in the spirit of the obedient man and the reason of his conduct. I can look back to a similar spiritualizing of our old Greek morality as stress was laid on the intent with which an act was done. But this man lifts such principles above mere ethics, sees them as final forms of the divine command. He draws two precepts from the Jewish law: "Thou shalt love the Lord thy God with all thy heart, and with all thy soul, and with all thy mind. This is the first and great commandment; And the second is like unto it, Thou shalt love thy neighbor as thyself. On these two commandments hang all the law and the prophets." This is indeed a spiritualizing of righteousness — of the entire contents of human conduct. He shows its application among men: "All things therefore whatsoever ye would that men should do unto you, even so do ye also unto them; for this is the law and the prophets." Our Stoicism was groping towards the love of God and man; but it lagged far behind the inspiration and command of these living words, which set the spirit of man's life and filled it with acts of love.

Then this man declared the outcome of such living and its reward to be life eternal — which is what men are looking for with all mortality's yearnings. *If only they could believe it!* As a disembodied spirit I could speak to them: but that is barred. Only I will here set down — is it for me? for whom is it? — how this doctrine was presented at its best and highest, and how it touched myself.

The man wrote nothing, but was always speaking to those about him; to his followers or to individuals, or to multitudes. When not angrily rejected, his teaching was accepted and afterwards recorded according to the tempers, spiritual aptitudes, and intelligence of his hearers. It survives in different forms. One is that of the kingdom of heaven for those who will believe and follow Christ — which he proclaimed himself to be. The Kingdom is set forth in images — parables, as they are called. These represent ways of God's redeeming love and the manner of man's acceptance of the Kingdom or failure to enter in. They are phases of the relationship between man and God, a relationship that may comprise the sum of human life. The teacher points to himself as the embodiment of the Kingdom of God and as the way to it.

Another record gives a profoundly complementary disclosure of the nature of life eternal. Its problems or dilemmas are put in statements that appeal to an educated and intellectual Greek, because of linkages with his philosophy. Such a one had learned that the life of mind is most desirable and that luxury and wealth might well be abandoned for it. We Greeks could understand the words: "Love not the world, neither the things that are in the world." Also the command laid on the disciples to love one another as the master had loved them, or even as God loved them. We who knew the great Athenian's philosophy could understand this. Now the discourse becomes profounder, esoteric perhaps, showing some likeness to what was taught in our own "mysteries." The Son of God was sent as an offer of eternal life: "For God so loved the world, that he gave his only begotten Son, that whosoever believeth on him should not perish, but have eternal life." Belief begins as the Father draws the man to Christ; it strengthens through the believer's love. Life is set forth as knowledge of the truth that frees man from bondage to sin and death; in fine, as knowing God and him whom He has sent. "This is life eternal, that they might know thee the only true God, and Jesus Christ whom thou has sent." The record contains further revelation of the believer's life in Christ and God: "That they may be one, even as we are one; I in them, and thou in me, that they may be perfected into one."

As I consider the tendencies of thought and feeling in the years before and those which followed the appearance of this man, I see how his teaching — the Gospel, as it came to be called — carried an answer and fulfillment to prevailing religious yearning. I who am a mind and soul reflecting men's fervent thoughts find my own religious feeling responded to and satisfied. The Stoic god was vague and material, and the thoughts on the divine held by the Athenian philosopher never quite reached a living focus. I needed personality in God, even though one built out of human aspirations. No living divine personality had ever been conceived such as was revealed in this Gospel set upon Jewish thought but reaching so far beyond. Besides this, some kind of imperishable existence is desired by all sorts of mortals. The Gospel promised it in promises snatched at and understood in many ways.

But the reasoning mind continued in Greeks and Greek-taught Romans — certainly in me. The Greek philosophic reason could not be so Judaized as to accept the Gospel as at first set forth. Its statements had to be made over in terms acceptable to Hellenic thought. So in my case. I followed sympathetically the disputes and labors of the Christian Fathers to make the relations between the divine Son and Father and mankind thinkable. These modes of Hellenized Christianity appealed to me and satisfied my philosophic nature.

What a fortune lay before these dogmas, in which the Gospel core lived on through its appeal to the hearts of men and women. Yet I, who feel the stirrings of what history would call the future time, already know that the reasonings of the Hellenic setting of the Gospel and the arguments of the mighty Apostle to the Gentiles will eventually lose the power to convince. For they will cease to correspond with any sense of reality present in men's minds.

V

For the time my religious feeling is satisfied by the Gospel of the Saviour Jesus Christ, and I accept its dogmatic rendering. My reason, unimpaired perhaps, is redirected by a faith that has made me introspective and furnished new matter to be fitted into an intellectual frame. I would never admit that we Greeks lacked the faculty of observing nature as well as man. The promptings of mathematics pushed us to discovery. Personally I have always been drawn to poetry and art and have done my thinking along the ways of reasoning rather than through observation. In my present state observation does not interest me. Mythology and religion find symbols and look for allegorical meanings in history. I may come to recognize that these images turn us from reality. But allegory will dominate the period into which our peoples are passing.

The turning of the world to Christianity is affecting intellectual taste as well as mood and feeling in another way. One would hardly call the Greeks unemotional. Passion inspired our art and swayed our history. But we never deified emotion, and looked always to its control. That it might be without limit and absolutely righteous did not occur to us. The Christian love of God is bringing a change. It is an overmastering emotion with those who feel it, and is deemed the essence of righteousness. No temperance, no μηδὲν ἄγαν here. The devoted soul cannot have too much of that which should embrace its entire nature. This boundless intellectual passion inspires the writings of the bishop of Hippo, whose genius I revere. I foresee the same passion moulding poetry and art. Our old Greek measures imposed emotional limit and control. They are dropped. The Christian hymn is taking on rhythms and rhymes which will gather power to express limitless yearning. Christian prose also will become emotional. Emotion will give new forms to poetry and new qualities to sculpture and painting.

Nevertheless, in these earlier centuries of conversion the masses of mankind go on much the same. They have merely redirected their superstitions. Is it not always so? The intellectually and spiritually chosen are sensitive to the impact of ideals originating in unique individuals or arising from human growth. From the first, such men were reinspired by the Gospel and gained in mental and emotional power. They reached new heights of righteousness — of intolerance, perhaps. Creative in thought and feeling, they are the great Fathers of the Church and saints as well. I feel their power. But I see that common men, with affections and desires good and bad, are unchanged. Wars go on, and internecine struggles among Christians still grasping at the Empire. The birth throes of dogma are violent enough, and bring forth subjects of rancorous dispute. Men hate each other still. I fail to see that bishops and their shouting factions are any better than pagans used to be. They are certainly less pleasant. Yet the tough old world may be about to receive a novel impress.

I am thinking of another aspect of this problem. Our antique world held much strength and life when Jesus was born. Its energies seemed to sink while his teachings, more or less altered, were reaching general acceptance. My own experience through this period of spiritual intermingling and renovation impresses me with the impossibility of distinguishing the causes of these two phenomena or even the phenomena themselves — to wit, the apparent weakening of Greco-Roman civilization and the Gospel's spread. Men are evincing new susceptibilities and capacities of feeling, which tend to develop into creative faculty, thus making amends for what is lost. The antique Greek and Roman character, although subject to superstitions, was strong and self-reliant. The staunchness relaxed under a deepening need of religious solace and support. This need brought forth the means of consolation. The times of the Church Fathers were creative of Christian art as well as Christian dogma. The Fathers themselves in the fourth century after Christ were not mentally inferior to Epicurus and the founders of Stoicism in the fourth century before his birth. Christian art was less skillful than the art of our Skopas and Praxiteles, but more original in its accomplishment of the novel task of presenting the Christian epic.

Thus I saw new elements of faculty and character replacing the antique strength. One hesitates to speak of a human deterioration. But disasters press upon my thought. I see the resources and population of the Empire wasted by war, disorder, and disease. The impact of barbarian peoples is now a calamity rather than a renewal of strength. Our civilization is no longer able to assimilate and fashion them.

VI

I am moved by the tendencies of each passing time, and yet consider them detachedly. This is my freedom. I see the world entering a period of downfall and ignorance to be followed by a gradual recovery rich in possibilities. The course of disruption and recovery passes across my vision. Through the centuries I hear the beat of thought and feel the gathering passion of the Faith. I think in terms of the *Summa theologiae* and almost gain the gift of tears. Then I become aware of a dawning freedom struggling through the need of the antique heritage. Eyes are opening to the natural world. Observation becomes active and experimental, prying into movement and growth. Religion holds a smaller part of human interest. Man's earthly life bounds forward as if unfettered. There is delight in art; and the passionately human world asserts itself with glorious violence in Shakespearean plays.

Moving on to what seems the present, I am dizzied by the novel facilities of daily life and intercourse. In the whirl of opportunity it is humanity that stays the same. What though men talk across the ocean if they have but small things to say? Inventions are a fool's test of progress.

The cry is for application and utility. But applied science is baneful as well as beneficial: neutral between good and ill. Easement and facility are well when leading to broader purpose and the uplifting of the mind. It is an insult to knowledge to accept surface utility as a criterion of its worth. We Greeks kept the balance between philosophy and science. Now the efficiency of rational thinking is denied. Men forget that in sifting nature perception is fashioned by the perceiving mind with the concurrence of its reasoning faculties. The gain is valid when harmonized with the background of well-considered thought. This court of last resort passes on every fact. Natural knowledge broadens the basis of that ultimate rational consideration which is philosophy.

Though the world perplexes me, I know whither I have come. A touch of the divine in the liberated soul enables it to see all things in the light of eternity. I can also view my own experiences as successive. With the passing of mortal breath, the distraction and contentions of composite existence gave way to quietude and gentle tolerance. I became hospitable to others' thoughts, would consider novel opinions and recognize new drifts of feeling. I absorbed the early philosophers and the laws of conduct declared by the Theban poet and our Athenian drama. Having soared with Plato, my thoughts were sobered as man's helplessness appeared in the times of Stoicism. The pathos of mortality brought home the need of divine deliverance. I gained a new intelligence from the conviction that God, once the All-mover, now the Father, held human qualities in the divine harmony of his nature. He had made us unto himself. There was scope along that path for human energies, and content and peace. Thus I fared onward. Insistence upon living within the divine purpose remains unshaken. I, Archilochus, have found the peace of God which passeth understanding. And I also am an allegory.

V

PLACING THE MIDDLE AGES

Placing the Middle Ages

I

THROUGHOUT human history the past is carried on in each succeeding present, yet without controlling what it helps to form. Some periods are creative or radically reconstructive; others appear to use their wits in capturing the heritage of thought and feeling offered by the past. Although the Middle Ages of Western Europe belong to this less originative type, they have their own character and achievement. My intention is to indicate briefly, in the way of suggestive illustration, some of the formative antecedents entering the Middle Ages; next, their treatment of what was received; and lastly the manner of their contribution to the store of human values.

The Gospel of Jesus was made over in the course of its progress among the various Mediterranean peoples. There were also shiftings of pagan thought and temper, changes in conceptions of fact and ways of regarding physical phenomena. This was the final reconstructive period of the antique world — but a world from the time of Constantine effectively converted to Christianity. The last does not mean that the inhabitants of the Roman Empire were spiritually renewed and uplifted. But it does mean that the creative energies of the time were dominated and directed by convictions springing from an acceptance of the Christian faith.

In the Hellenic East as well as in the Latin West, the Fathers drew their education from the antique culture, of which they still made part. Naturally their ways of thinking and of conceiving any and every kind of fact were affected by the current modes of pagan thought. But they maintained that in pagan learning they sought only a broader light upon their faith. It should be used, as Origen said, with Christianity as an end. Theology was the chief patristic pursuit. Here the Latins, following the leadership of the East, reset in their own tongue the Nicaean formulation. Within this frame they rounded out their religion in doctrine and practice. They were more constructive as ecclesiastical organizers. The Roman Catholic Church which was to uphold and extend the Christian domination of the West, was the creation of the Latin genius.

Neo-Platonism represents the chief refashioning of Greek philosophy which accompanied the patristic refashioning of Christianity. With its founder, Plotinus, it was a prodigious system of metaphysics, and yet looked beyond dialectic to a goal of ecstatic union with God. This goal was religious and mystic because, while unattainable through reason, it could be won by an exalted intuition. The successors of Plotinus, with less strenuous minds, accepted all manner of theurgic magic as means of access to the divine. Compared with the temper of Plato's or Aristotle's teaching, Neo-Platonism showed as profound a change in mood and feeling as in thought.

There were affinities between Neo-Platonism and Christianity. Plotinus may have been influenced by those Platonic Alexandrine Fathers, Clement and Origen; and Christian circles might be touched with Neo-Platonism and other ways of pagan thinking. But, fixed in the Gospel conviction of salvation through the God-man, Jesus Christ, the Faith proved mightier than them all. Though the Fathers used Greek philosophic thinking, they repudiated many of its conclusions; and the formation of the Faith gained clarity and distinctness through rejection of aberrations rooted in paganism. The course of rejection and adaptation may be indicated by the names of Tertullian and Origen, both somewhat older than Plotinus; then Athanasius, Basil, the Greek Gregories; for the Latin West, Ambrose, Jerome, Hilary, Augustine, the last dying in the year 430. There follows a century and a half of barbarization and darkening mental vision, and we note the name of the great pope Gregory, who died in 604. Before then, in 529, the Emperor Justinian had struck the death knell of pagan philosophy by closing its schools at Athens.

Latin Christianity was completed in the person and work of Augustine. Through him the lines of religious thinking were set for the coming centuries of western Christendom. And first among the Fathers he gave utterance to religious feeling in eternal forms. His own conversion and later religious growth reflect the ways by which Latin Christianity had become what it was when his life-work closed. The appeal of the Saviour, which had drawn the pagan masses, drew Augustine. Acceptance of Christ extricated him from the mazes of other beliefs. Yet his Christian faith was clothed in reasonings of latter-day Platonism, which entered Latin Christianity through this greatest of Latin Fathers.

Surely there had been devoted love of Jesus from the beginning. But the patristic mind, both Greek and Latin, was engaged in the formulation and establishment of dogma. Here also worked the genius of Augustine, but ever with the love of God pressing to utterance. Augustine's love had its anxieties; but Pope Gregory the Great and not Augustine was to be the founder of the terror-stricken medieval fear of hell. The trenchant side of Augustine's nature stood out as he became a church dignitary and the chief doctrinal authority of his time, with all manner of controversial exigencies pressing on him. Here again, his own career paralleled the growth and organization of the Roman Catholic Church. None more than he helped to make firm the principle that the Church was the final doctrinal authority and the sole vessel of Christian salvation.

So the Gospel was set in dogma formed through ways of pagan thought *converted* to its support. Quite as masterfully, pagan culture was made to serve the Faith. One can hardly overestimate the adaptive and creative energy of these patristic centuries, which set the foundations of medieval growth. By extending the period to the death of Gregory in 604, we see how complete was both the work itself and its effect upon the Middle Ages. The Catholic Church was established as the sole and universal religious authority. The sum of dogma was made up. The allegorical interpretation of scripture was set forth and accepted — culminating, as it did, in Pope Gregory's Commentary on the Book of Job, which veritably became the Job of the Middle Ages. In these same centuries the pattern of the perfect Christian life was fixed in a monasticism ordered by the *Regula* of St. Benedict of Nursia, who died in 543. Before then the imperial triumph of the Faith had evoked a burst of creative Christian art. On the walls of the newly built churches the whole Christian and pre-Christian story was rendered in mosaics. With no models to copy, but doubtless under ecclesiastical direction, the artists of the fourth and fifth centuries set type-patterns which were to be followed in the Middle Ages and the Renaissance. As for secular education, the rudiments were handed on in the grammars of Donatus and Priscian and the works of Boethius and Cassiodorus. A more debased pagan knowledge was preserved in the everlastingly quoted *Etymologies* of Archbishop Isidore of Seville, a younger contemporary of Pope Gregory.

Such then was the heritage of the Middle Ages. Next, the people who were to receive it. Fashioned within the circle of the Roman Empire, it had to be presented to the heathen beyond the pale. Its effect on them depended on their own qualities and a chastening awe regarding what was indeed a gospel of Latin civilization. There had never been a lack of contacts between Rome and a barbarism always filtering or breaking in, or shaken by the impact of Roman conquest. As Rome weakened, the broken functions of government passed to the Church. It was to be her office to turn the heathen to Christianity and civilization. So Pope Gregory sent one who was to become St. Augustine of Canterbury to convert a heathen England. This was in 577. A century earlier, in a disordered but still Latin Gaul, Clovis the Frank was baptized a Catholic Christian, an event of import for him and the troubled world. Decades pass, and a St. Willibord, under the authority of the pope and the protection of Charles Martel, converts the Frisians, and his greater disciple, St. Boniface-Winfried, becomes the apostle to Germany beyond the Rhine.

Gaul, already a land of partially Latinized Christians, was to hold a mediatorial role between Latindom and the outer barbaric world. Provence was quite Latin, and, like Italy, showed a decadence that was apt to join hands with barbarism on a common level. Antique custom and tradition hung over these lands and, at least in Italy, the surviving power of the antique clogged the growth of distinctively medieval thought and literary form, and impeded the rise of any great style of church architecture. The heart and soul and mind of medieval growth was to be the less deeply Latinized and mediatorial France. That country and neighboring northern lands, rather than Italy, show the manner of the medieval appropriation of the antique Christian heritage and the genius of the Middle Ages.

II

The crude conversion of Teuton peoples and their contact with Latin letters bring the factors of medieval growth into conjunction. Medieval culture, and indeed the medieval genius, issued from their combined action, rather than from the particular effect of any one of them. The conjunction was well under way when, in 771, the greatest of medieval rulers became the sole sovereign of the vast Merovingian realm. In so far as the Middle Ages had not already begun, they assuredly open with Charlemagne. His arms and mighty ordering prevailed against Saxons, Avars, Bavarians, Slavs, Danes, Lombards. He conquered northern Italy, freed the pope, and in the year 800 revived in himself the name of Emperor. Justice was made firm and new roads opened to trade. Churches were established and religion uplifted in his realm. He promoted Latin studies, sacred and profane, enlisted the best teachers, and became an eager learner. Early in his reign he met the Anglo-Saxon Alcuin, and attached him to himself to be thenceforth his most trusted director of education.

The educational needs were elementary, and the teaching equally so. Although a few scholars could write grammatical Latin and make apt verses, there was call to teach the rudiments of diction. Alcuin drew from Donatus, Priscian, or Isidore the materials for his *Grammar and Orthography* and his *Rhetoric*, composed in dialogue form, simple works, occasionally childlike. His *De dialectica* was still cruder, because logic is more difficult than grammar, and so was another stage above his powers.

Alcuin also shared in the labor for which the teaching of Latin was preparatory. The object was to understand the Christian faith. The works of the Fathers offered the means. Based on Scripture, they were necessarily an interpretation of it. But the patristic compositions were the fruit of a mentality above the Carolingian age. Their contents had to be rearranged under plain and pointed headings. An obvious way was to paragraph the matter, and attach it to the proper verse. Thus a true understanding of Scripture could be had. Some of the patristic work was in this form, notably Pope Gregory's Commentary on Job. Gregory's interpretations, like those of the Fathers before him, were mostly allegorical. This method led the Middle Ages captive, and allegory became the chief field for the medieval imagination. But the Carolingian age neither had nor desired originality. Exhaustive compilations from the Fathers were made by Alcuin's Teutonic pupil, Rabanus Maurus, and were brought to a finish by the skill of *his* pupil, Walafrid Strabo, whose *Glossa ordinaria* continued in use for centuries.

Rabanus' labors won him the title of *Primus praeceptor Germaniae*, made him abbot of Fulda and eventually archbishop of Mainz. While knowledge of Scripture remained his sum of wisdom, he had a better understanding of grammar, logic, and the other Arts, than Alcuin. He saw that logic was the discipline which enabled teacher and learner to detect error and discover truth. After him scholarship continued to improve, though it still was mainly compilation. Only controversies on points where the Fathers were obscure made these compilers think for themselves. Sometimes they repointed the patristic arguments effectively, so as to give the conclusion the force of a projectile, as Radpertus Paschasius, abbot of Corbie, did with the Eucharist in his *De corpore et sanguine Domini*.

A younger man belonging to the ninth century had indeed his own way of thinking, which would have been more vehemently condemned had its implications been perceived. This was the Irishman, John Scotus Eriugena, who knew Greek as well as Latin. He translated into Latin the *Celestial Hierarchy* of Pseudo-Dionysius, and drew from it draughts of Neo-Platonism for his book *De divisione naturae*. In this truly constructive work, he displayed the logic which he loved and relied on; and even stated the principle, not too conspicuously, that reason should be set above authority. The first to use old material with original power, he heads the line of recalcitrant, often heretical, medieval thinkers.

These are some slight suggestions of the beginnings of medieval culture. Scholarship advanced as generations of northern men in France, in England, and in German lands along the Rhine studied Latin grammar and read the classics. A lover of all learning was the prodigious Gerbert, who, born in Aquitaine about 950, passed some student years in Spain, and then taught the entire range of academic discipline at the episcopal school of Rheims. In the course of a troubled career, through the merited favor of three imperial Ottos, he became abbot of Bobbio, archbishop of Rheims and later of Ravenna, and at last Pope Sylvester II, in the year 999. A marvelous story of one who pursued all knowledge — logic, arithmetic, astronomy, as well as letters; who reflected the thoughts of Cicero, and collected manuscripts as ardently as any man of the *quattrocento*.

One of Gerbert's pupils became a great teacher, Fulbert, bishop of Chartres from 1006 to 1028. Chartres had long been a center of learning: Fulbert made it the chief cathedral school of France. The courses in grammar and rhetoric were extended; logic was followed through the simpler Aristotelian treatises; and better instruction was given in the four branches of the Quadrivium, arithmetic, geometry, music and astronomy, for which Gerbert had done much.

So Latin studies were well under way by the eleventh century. In the twelfth, medieval Latin reached its highest literary excellence; all of which represents the genial appropriation of antique culture. We turn to its complement, the appropriation of patristic Christianity. Promoted by acquaintance with the classics, this phase of medieval development proceeded with the maturing of the medieval peoples. Its course followed the patristic matter, and was guided by the unavoidable use of Greek philosophy, Neo-Platonism, roughly speaking, in the twelfth century and the new Aristotle in the thirteenth. The task was to comprehend, rearrange, and finally reformulate the subject with little substantial origination.

The system, which we call Scholasticism, was formal, since its constant effort was to formulate; it was rational, because logic was its soul. It was humble in the presence of its two great sources, the Fathers and the philosophers. Scholasticism was, above all, theology. In it faith stood first; as Augustine said, *credimus ut cognoscamus*, we believe in order that we may know. But there were troubling divergences, beginning with Eriugena's setting reason above authority; passing on through Abélard's prickly thinking; abutting at last on Roger Bacon's dangerous emphasizing of observation and experiment. Still the priority of faith and the unquestioned supremacy of the goal of salvation directed and controlled scholastic currents.

We mark three stages in the development of this theological philosophy. First, the learning of the patristic matter, the stage of the Carolingian Scripture commentaries, already noticed. It corresponded with elementary grammatical studies. In the eleventh century, logic advances, another branch of the Trivium; and the simpler Aristotelian treatises are mastered. This discipline promotes the second stage of Scholasticism, represented by the books of Sentences — chief among them *Sententiarum libri quatuor* of Peter Lombard, who died bishop of Paris in 1160. Winding its way through scriptural and patristic citations, largely from Augustine, the Lombard's work proceeds methodically and logically, stating the proposition, giving the authorities in its support and then those which differ, and ending with a conciliating or distinguishing statement of the approved result. Very little philosophy is brought in beyond that contained in the statements of Augustine.

In the decades following the Lombard's death, the complete logical *Organon* of Aristotle became known through Latin translations; and gradually the entire body of the Master's substantial philosophy. It was this that was to be learned and mastered, and finally employed, in a complete and organic presentation of the Christian scheme of salvation. The prodigious achievement was mainly the work of three men, the creators of that scholastic triumph, the *Summa theologiae*. All of them, some time in their careers, taught at Paris. First, the Franciscan, Alexander of Hales, who died in 1245, gathers the material together, retaining the order of the Lombard's Sentences. But he enlarged his matter in the conclusion or *resolutio*, which followed the statement of each proposition and the counter arguments. Then came the two Dominican Colossi, Albertus Magnus and Thomas Aquinas. Albert, son of a noble German house, was born at the close of the twelfth century, spent his long life in study and ecclesiastical administration, and died in 1280. He lived, however, to defend the doctrines of his great pupil after the latter's death in 1274. Thomas was born in southern Italy of princely Swabian and Norman stocks, domiciled for some generations in that land which seemed to lend its invaders the faculty of form.

The *Summa theologiae* issued from the hand of Thomas a finished monument, into which was built all pertinent

Aristotelian material to support and expand the Christian scheme of salvation. As related to its medieval preparation, it rested on the previous mastery of Aristotelian logic. The interplay of intellectual activity in the universities had part in it. But specifically it was made possible through the extension of metaphysics and natural knowledge coming from the comprehensive study of Aristotle. It is this that distinguishes the writings of Albertus Magnus from any composition of the twelfth century. He had gone beyond the natural knowledge and philosophy preserved in Boethius and the Fathers, and had penetrated as effectively as the Latin translations permitted to a primary Greek source.[1] The work of his pupil included whatever Albert's teaching afforded as training and material, and was based on a surer knowledge of Aristotle from better translations, probably supervised by himself. Out of all this, with transcendent genius, Thomas produced a unified and organic work, which set forth the nature of God, so far as man might comprehend it, unfolded the creature world corporeal and spiritual, and presented the nature of man, his relationship to God, and his eternal lot. The all-considering mind of Thomas omitted nothing and left nothing at loose ends. The scheme was consistent, rational, and complete.

The progress of Scholasticism as an unbroken whole ended with Thomas. His contemporary, Roger Bacon,

[1] A parallel return to a great source was the recovery of the *Digest* of Justinian, the classic compilation of Roman jurisprudence in its best period, the second and third centuries of our era. The medieval preparation for an understanding of the *Digest* presents analogies with the stages in the appropriation of other portions of the antique heritage.

made an abortive attack upon its methods and the soundness of its knowledge. And, before many decades passed, Duns Scotus more fatally assailed the union of philosophy based on human reason and theology set upon divine revelation. Arguing against Thomas for the primacy of the will over the intellect, he maintained that theology was not a speculative science but a practical guide. After him, Occam showed more trenchantly that faith did not depend on knowledge, and that the truths of revelation neither needed nor admitted the proofs of reason.

Scholasticism expresses the chief and, as one may say, the ultimate intellectual interest of the Middle Ages. Its achievement consisted in the assimilation of antique and patristic themes and their restatement in a new and noble form. There was slight philosophic originality and but a meager extension of natural science, to which the medieval contribution was unimportant. Moreover, while Scholasticism might take its rational measure of the impulsive and mystic soul, it was not palpably expressive of religious feeling.

But human nature has other faculties than the intellectual. The mind may act on impulse, upon intuitions and convictions not reached through reason. Philosophy is troubled to define these activities which sound in feeling and move through emotion. But theirs has been a creative role in religion and art, as well as in daily life and love. Perhaps the most significant evolution of lasting human values in the Middle Ages did not lie in Scholasticism. Rather, its source was feeling and emotion functioning through other phases of the mind or stirring them to effective action.

The focus of medieval emotional growth was religious. It took form and direction from the gradually transformed patristic Christianity, in which worked the intellectual energies of the time. Reflection upon this saving scheme rapidly filled with gratitude for the promised salvation and love for the crucified Saviour. As is the way with emotion, this love and gratitude pressed to utterance, and, feeding upon its expression, gained in power. Thus seeking ever more facile and adequate modes of expression, the religious passion of the Middle Ages compelled the medieval intelligence to join with it in the creation of effective and beautiful forms. They seem to me as original and vital as the *Summa theologiae*. The medieval imagination flowered in divers human and fantastic shapes. But the primal source was the emotional nature of men and women potently expanding with the emotionalizing of their religion.

The evolution of fitting forms followed the growth of religious feeling. First we mark the impassioning of devotional Latin prose, as with Peter Damiani and St. Anselm in the eleventh century, then its vibrant culmination in St. Bernard. His sermons have rhyming sentences that might be recast as hymns. A simpler gospel feeling fills the early "lives" of St. Francis, whose life was a poem.

Yet prose is a halting vehicle for feeling, which always seeks, and will create, the chanted strophe. At an early period, Christian verse dropped the simple meters of St. Ambrose. Following the usages of daily speech, it turned to accentual lines, soon to be equipped with rhyme. Some verse forms emerged from antique moulds; but the mighty medieval hymn sprang from the need and faculty of sacred song. The Sequence is my illustration. Literally it grew out of the cadenced chanting of the final *a* in the Alleluia chorus of the Mass, by means of the substitution of sonorous words for that closing *a*. These were gradually made into verses, which followed the evolution of musical melody and promoted it. Out of this melody and song emerged the splendid hymns of Adam of St. Victor, greatest of medieval hymn writers. He dwelt in the convent of St. Victor on the left bank of the Seine, not far from Notre Dame. Lovely songs and poems as they were, his hymns followed the lines of medieval orthodoxy, as they glorified the saints and reveled in scriptural allegories taken from the quivers of the Church Fathers.

Allegory also frames the lurid passion of the visions of ascetic women. In these, as in the hymns, it gains new feeling, a new life indeed, and then enters all phases of medieval thinking. Its spirit moved one twelfth-century philosopher to construct a symbolic universe. Never man thought more deeply in this medium than Hugo, also of St. Victor. Reflecting upon the symbolism of the sacraments, he enlarged his argument to a demonstration of the symbolical nature of God's entire creation. The true reality of all things lies in their symbolical meaning. Hugo's thoughts, through his disciple Richard, pass into that final realistic allegory of the pilgrim soul, the *Divina Commedia*.

Religious art carries a like story of the emotionalizing of the patristic matter through a poignant vitalizing of allegory. The stately mosaics that by the sixth century covered the walls of the newly risen basilicas, while antique in style, were a prodigy of inventive design. But they had been too recently and correctly composed to carry the qualities of love and fear and pity. Many of the sacred themes were carried on, some without radical change. In the early Middle Ages art was too decadent and barbarous to do them justice. Only as the thirteenth century closes comes Giotto with his greater skill and dramatic genius. His frescoes tell the whole Christian story animated and humanized with love and pity, as one finds it on the walls of Santa Maria del Arena in Padua. His pupils in Rome imbue even their mosaics with a new feeling, absent from the art of the fifth century.

The great cathedral art of France sheds a still broader illumination on our theme. Sculpture and glass painting give the Christian and pre-Christian story, and link it with the active life of man on earth. Yet the drama of man's creation, fall, redemption, and final judgment is presented in the profoundest reality of its symbolic character. The power of this art proves that the artist craftsman thought and felt within his allegory. In matchless symbolism his art rises to the ideal, as it portrays, not the natural human form, but the beauty of the human spirit under the power and grace of God.

Besides its glass and sculpture, the church itself, emerging from dumb barrel-vaulting, has made its aisles, its arches and windows and its flying buttresses express the passionate aspiration of the soul. Architecture itself is emotionalized in Gothic churches.

The scholastic and religious energies of the Middle Ages seem to me the core of medieval development. This central intellectual and emotional activity, with its increasing knowledge and expanding feeling, moved human faculties other than religious, and affected the literature of this world. Allegory passed into secular writings; it made the structure of the most popular of vernacular poems, the *Roman de la rose*, and countless others. It played its part in politics, furnishing many an argument in the conflict between the Empire and the Papacy. In the medieval imagination ideas moved, as of course, from symbol to symbol.

The Christian faith demanded that the love of God should dominate the mind and soul of the believer. This principle enlarged the human capacity for loving and gave a new power to the loves of men and women. Despite all monkish precepts, love's worth and sovereignty were recognized not merely in romantic literature but occasionally in life, as witness the love of Héloïse for Abélard. Love's virtue puts an *intelligenza nuova* in the heart to lift it up in tears. Behind the *Commedia* is the sonnet-text:

> Intelligenza nuova che l'Amore
> Piangendo mette in lui, pur su lo tira.

So it was that in the centuries of medieval culmination, scholars, theologians, poets, and artist-craftsmen worked and wrought in the antique and patristic material which had been less masterfully used by men before them. Through the discipline and prompting of what had become part of their natures, they created much that was their own. They formed a consistent and rational system of theology, which included human knowledge and human life. They drew from it fear and pity and a passionate love of Christ. Then thoughts which had learned to pant and quiver gave themselves to mortal love.

Medieval men sought to think and imagine in unbroken patterns and whole schemes. The goal should still be a *summa*, but a *summa* of the heart as well as of the mind. The *Divina Commedia* is such a *summa*, and likewise a Gothic cathedral. *Commedia* and Cathedral, as well as the *Summa theologiae*, carry on the elements of their preparation. Through the labor of making their inheritance their own, the Middle Ages produced whatever of lasting value it was their fortune to hand on. No period of history shows more clearly how little of what goes before is lost in the most signal creations of the human spirit.